WARS OF THE 20th CENTURY

Also in this series (available at Amazon.com):

- Wars of the 20th Century – Volume 2: Twenty Wars That Shaped the Present World

- Wars of the 20th Century – Volume 3: Twenty Wars That Shaped the Present World

- Wars of the 20th Century – Volume 4: Twenty Wars That Shaped the Present World

WARS OF THE 20th CENTURY

Twenty Wars That Shaped the Present World

DANIEL ORR

Cover photo *(in the public domain)*: Communist troops at the Battle of Siping during the Chinese Civil War. 1946.

ISBN – 13: 978-1499738728
ISBN – 10: 1499738722

CONTENTS

LIST OF MAPS ---vii

PREFACE --xi

CAMBODIAN CIVIL WAR--1

VIETNAMESE INVASION OF CAMBODIA ---------------------------------7

CHINESE CIVIL WAR--13

LANDING OPERATION ON HAINAN ISLAND --------------------------27

ANGLO-AFGHAN WAR OF 1919---31

1947-1948 CIVIL WAR IN PALESTINE ----------------------------------35

1948 ARAB-ISRAELI WAR--43

BOSNIAN WAR---51

KOSOVO WAR ---59

NAGORNO-KARABAKH WAR--65

FIRST CONGO WAR--73

SECOND CONGO WAR---79

ANGOLAN WAR OF INDEPENDENCE ----------------------------------89

ANGOLAN CIVIL WAR --103

UNITED STATES OCCUPATION OF NICARAGUA --------------117

NICARAGUAN REVOLUTION (1961 - 1979) AND COUNTER-REVOLUTION (1981 - 1990) --123

FOOTBALL WAR--133

DIRTY WAR--139

CHACO WAR ---145

1932 SALVADORAN PEASANT UPRISING --------------------------153

BIBLIOGRAPHY---159

INDEX---171

LIST OF MAPS

Map 1. Indo-China region during the Cambodian Civil War (1970-1975)..2

Map 2. Vietnamese Invasion of Cambodia. Political unrest in the Indo-China region led to many wars, the most famous being the Vietnam War. In 1975, two communist countries in Indo-China went to war, with Vietnam launching an invasion of Kampuchea (Cambodia)...............9

Map 3. China's two major river systems, Yellow River and Yangtze River, served as strategic battle lines between communist and nationalist forces during the latter stages of the Chinese Civil War. 17

Map 4. China's provinces that were affected during the Chinese Civil War. 19

Map 5. China's cities that were affected during the Chinese Civil War. Nationalist forces under Chiang Kai-shek retreated to the island of Taiwan (lower right) after their defeat in the war. 24

Map 6. Hainan Island in southern China. In April 1950, Chinese communist forces from the Leizhou Peninsula crossed Hainan Strait and invaded Hainan. After three weeks of fighting, Nationalist forces defending the island were defeated. 29

Map 7. Anglo-Afghan War of 1919. The British Empire's prized possession during the nineteenth and twentieth centuries was the Indian subcontinent. Afghanistan served as a neutral zone between the region's two major powers, the Russian Empire and the British Empire. 33

Map 8. United Nations Partition Plan for Palestine. The original plan released by the UN proposed to allocate 56% of Palestine to Jews, while 43% would be allotted to Palestinian Arabs. Jerusalem, at 1% of the territory, would be administered by the UN (map redrawn after Morris, 2008). 40

Map 9. 1947-1948 Civil War in Palestine. Some key combat areas are shown..41

Map 10. 1948 Arab-Israeli War. Key battle areas are shown. The Arab countries of Egypt, Jordan, Syria, Lebanon, and Iraq, assisted by volunteer fighters from other Arab states, invaded newly formed Israel that had occupied a sizable portion of Palestine..........................46

Map 11. The 1948 Arab-Israeli War. Palestine and adjacent countries are shown, as are the West Bank and the Gaza Strip....................................48

Map 12. Bosnian War. Some key battle sites are indicated. Serbia and Croatia, adjacent countries to Bosnia, were involved in the war since a sizable population of ethnic Croats and ethnic Serbs lived in Bosnia-Herzegovina...56

Map 13. Kosovo War. By using guerilla tactics, Kosovar insurgents gained control of portions of Kosovo (see text)...63

Map 14. Armenia and Azerbaijan. The two countries fought a war over the Nagorno-Karabakh region..67

Map 15. Nagorno-Karabakh. Some key battle sites during the Nagorno-Karabakh War. 69

Map 16. Africa showing location of the Democratic Republic of the Congo (DRC) and other African countries. At the time of the First Congo War, DRC was then known as Zaire. 75

Map 17. First Congo War. In the map D.R.C. refers to the Democratic Republic of the Congo..76

Map 18. Second Congo War. 84

Map 19.Africa showing location of present-day Angola and other African countries that were involved in the Angolan War of Independence. South-West Africa (present-day Namibia) was then under South African rule. 92

Map 20. Angolan War of Independence. Major areas of military operations by Angolan nationalist militias as well as by expeditionary forces from Zaire, South Africa, and Cuba. 99

Map 21. Angolan Civil War. The exclave Angolan province of Cabinda is shown at the top left..107

Map 22. Central America: Belize, Guatemala, Honduras, El Salvador, Nicaragua, Costa Rica, and Panama. Mexico, on the north, forms part of North America, while Colombia, on the south and east, belongs to South America..119

Map 23. Nicaragua. The U.S. decision to invade Nicaragua in 1912 was due, at least in part, to the American government's concern that another foreign power would build and then control the Nicaragua Canal. The United States regarded the whole Western Hemisphere as its exclusive sphere of influence. The Nicaragua Canal was intended to be a shipping waterway that connects the Pacific Ocean and Caribbean Sea. 121

Map 24. Nicaraguan Revolution (1961-1979). Communist rebels called Sandinistas fought to overthrow the autocratic regime of Anastacio Somoza. The Somoza dynasty ended when the rebels captured Managua, Nicaragua's capital. 127

Map 25. Football War. In 1969, El Salvador launched military operations inside Honduras. The areas affected by the war are indicated. 137

Map 26. Argentina and nearby countries. During the Dirty War, the Argentine government used "dirty" methods in its anti-insurgency campaign to stamp out leftist and perceived communist elements in the country. 141

Map 27. North Chaco (shaded) was the scene of a territorial war between Paraguay and Bolivia in the 1930s. 147

Map 28. Chaco War. Battle sites in the Chaco region and eastern Bolivia. 151

Map 29. 1932 Salvadoran Peasant Uprising. El Salvador's western region was the center of civilian unrest arising from the country's socio-economic inequalities. 156

PREFACE

This book presents twenty wars that took place in the twentieth century. The chronologically earliest of these wars was the 1912 U.S. Invasion and Occupation of Nicaragua, while the last to take place was the Second Congo War, which broke out in 1998 and ended in 2003, that is, early in the twenty-first century.

Presented are wars from the four major geographical entities, i.e. Europe, Asia, Africa, and the Americas, as well as different types of wars, e.g. independence wars, civil wars, political/ideological wars, ethnic/sectarian wars, etc. Some of these wars are fairly well known, such as the Arab-Israeli Wars and Bosnian War, although many others in this book are little-known and even obscure. For instance, the average person probably would not have heard of the Football War, Dirty War, or Chaco War.

The book was written in regular, non-technical language with the general readership in mind, and purposed to be used as a casual, everyday read or a convenient source of information to expand one's knowledge on a specific country's military history. For convenience only, the reader may wish to read through the book using the chapter sequence as presented, since some of the wars follow a chronological order. For example, the two wars in Palestine featured in this book (1947-1948 Civil War in Palestine, 1948 Arab-Israeli War) are sequenced one after the other. Alternatively, the reader may choose to jump to any topic of his or her interest, as each of the wars was written as a stand-alone article with no prior knowledge assumed.

The author now invites the reader to begin exploring the pages of this book.

CAMBODIAN CIVIL WAR

Between 1970 and 1975, the U.S.-backed government in Cambodia fought a civil war against the Khmer Rouge, a Cambodian insurgent movement that wanted to establish a communist regime in the country. The Khmer Rouge's victory in the war marked the rise into power of its leader, Pol Pot, who would engineer one of the bloodiest genocides in history. The civil war formed a part of the complex geopolitical theaters of tumultuous Indo-China during the first half of the 1970s, more particularly in reference to the Vietnam War which greatly affected the security climates of adjacent countries, including Cambodia (Map 1).

Background In 1970, serious economic problems in Cambodia prompted the military to overthrow Prince Norodom Sihanouk, Cambodia's ruling monarch, whose faulty policies led to widespread discontent among the people. Prince Sihanouk, although extremely popular and revered as a semi-deity by Cambodians, applied a calculating but dangerous foreign policy of playing up the superpowers in order to get the best deal for Cambodia, and still maintain neutrality.

Years earlier, Prince Sihanouk willingly had received military and financial assistance from the United States. But in 1965, after deciding that communism ultimately would prevail in Indo-China, he opened diplomatic relations with China and North Vietnam. Furthermore, he accepted military and economic support from North Vietnam. In return, he allowed the North Vietnamese Army to use sections of eastern Cambodia in its war against South Vietnam.

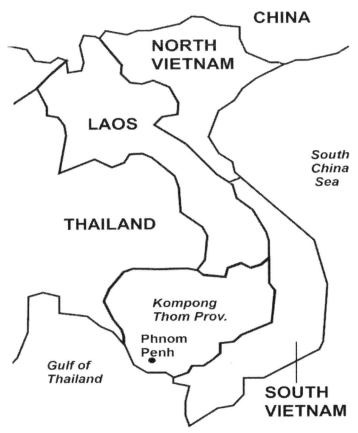

Map 1. The Indo-China region during the Cambodian Civil War (1970-1975).

The Vietnamese presence in Cambodia, however, fueled the centuries-old acrimonious relationship between the Cambodian people against their eastern neighbors. Anti-Vietnamese protests broke out in Phnom Penh, Cambodia's capital. Consequently, in 1970, military leaders and top government officials deposed Prince Sihanouk, who was away from the country at that time.

Prince Sihanouk did not return to Cambodia, but sought and was granted sanctuary in China. The coup's leader, Prime Minister Lon

Nol, established a government that wanted to keep Cambodia from any involvement in the Vietnam War.

But as the Vietnam War continued to spill over into Cambodia, Lon Nol turned to his traditional backer, the United States, which began to infuse his regime with large amounts of military and financial assistance. With the American money, Cambodia built a huge army, composed mainly of fanatical recruits who held anti-Vietnamese sentiments. Lon Nol's regime was weak, however, and the military was plagued with corruption and ineptitude. Cambodian forces also lacked combat experience. These factors would prove fatal in the coming war.

Operating from the Cambodian northeast mountains, the Khmer Rouge was an unknown insurgent group that wanted to turn Cambodia into a communist state. After being endorsed by the deposed Sihanouk (who wanted to return to power) and provided weapons by China, the Khmer Rouge quickly grew in numbers, power, and influence.

War In the early years of the civil war (1970-1972), the Khmer Rouge had little military capability. During this time, its battles against the Cambodian government were fought mainly by their North Vietnamese allies, who were also alarmed by Lon Nol's pro-American regime in Cambodia.

In May 1970, a large North Vietnamese Army offensive captured a sizable portion of eastern Cambodia. The attack came to within 15 miles of Phnom Penh before being driven back by the Cambodian Army. The following month, American and South Vietnamese army units counter-attacked and drove the North Vietnamese farther away to the north.

In June, the North Vietnamese attacked again, this time capturing the entire northeastern third section of the country, which they subsequently turned over to the Khmer Rouge for occupation and control. In April 1971, the Cambodian Army launched its only large offensive of the war, taking the northern city of Kompong Thom that had fallen earlier to the communists. In December, however, the city was retaken by the Khmer rebels, which they then held for the rest of the war.

By 1972, the Khmer Rouge had assembled an army of 35,000 full-time soldiers and 100,000 irregulars. It received massive military support from China, directed its own battles, and was completely self-reliant. The North Vietnamese turned over operational command to the Khmer Rouge and then withdrew from Cambodia, in order to fight is own war against South Vietnam. At this time, relations between Prince Sihanouk and the Khmer Rouge soured because of ideological differences. The Khmer rebels also wanted to rule Cambodia themselves and not reinstate the former ruler.

By early 1973, the Khmer Rouge was more than a match for the Cambodian Army. The Khmer rebels cut off communication lines north and south of Phnom Penh and began their advance toward the capital. Only a massive aerial bombardment of their positions by American warplanes saved Phnom Penh, forcing the rebels to flee back to the countryside.

By June 1973, however, the Khmer Rouge, after capturing many other Cambodian regions, held over 60% of the country. And by January 1975, as American military involvement in Indo-China was winding down, the Khmer rebels had encircled Phnom Penh and were starting the final assault on the capital. By this time, the city had fallen into chaos, with thousands of refugees from the countryside swelling the urban population. A serious food shortage occurred, as well as a spike in the prices of household commodities. Government services, such as education, health care, and shelter and relief, broke down.

The roads and waterways to the capital were blocked by the rebels, increasing the city's plight. Desertions in the Cambodian Army were widespread. In late March 1975, the remaining loyal government forces made a last stand as the numerically superior Khmer Rouge fought its way into the city. In the next few days, top Cambodian government officials and the remaining U.S. personnel fled the country. On April 17, 1975, Phnom Penh fell to the Khmer Rouge, which shortly thereafter formed a new communist government under Pol Pot.

.

VIETNAMESE INVASION OF CAMBODIA

On Christmas Day 1978, Vietnamese forces launched an invasion of Cambodia. Within two weeks, they had defeated the Cambodian Army and had overthrown the Khmer Rouge, Cambodia's Maoist government. Vietnam then installed a Marxist government in Cambodia that was allied to itself.

Background The origin of the war can be traced back as far as the 1200s when the Vietnamese invaded the region that now forms Cambodia and attempted to replace the local culture with its own. Then in the 1600s, through migration, the Vietnamese occupied and gained control of the sparsely populated eastern region of Cambodia that today constitutes the southern region of Vietnam. These events helped sow the seeds of ethnic tensions between Cambodia and Vietnam.

Then during the 1970s, Indo-China's charged political and security climate further aggravated this historical animosity, as the Cambodians believed that the Vietnamese planned to dominate and take control of the whole Indo-China region.

During the 1940s, communist movements were founded in Vietnam and Cambodia during the period of French colonization. These communist movements functioned in close association, with the Vietnamese communists leading and training their Cambodian counterparts. In the 1950s, after the French were defeated and subsequently withdrew from Indo-China, Vietnam was partitioned by the Geneva Peace Accords into North Vietnam, which became led by a communist regime, and South Vietnam, which formed a democratic government. Also in compliance with the Geneva Peace Accords, the Vietnamese forces pulled out of Cambodia. The Vietnamese communists espoused the Marxist-Leninist brand of communism, while the Cambodians were Maoist communists. The Cambodian communists were called Khmer Rouge and were led by Pol Pot, who later murdered millions of his people in one of the bloodiest genocides in history.

Both revolutionary movements triumphed in April 1975, with the Khmer Rouge overthrowing the U.S.-backed Cambodian government, and the Vietnamese communists entering Saigon, ending the American-sponsored South Vietnamese regime, and uniting the country under a Marxist government.

War The apparent communist solidarity between Vietnam and Cambodia was superficial, however, for as early as 1973 even before they had won their revolutions, the Khmer Rouge regularly ambushed North Vietnamese patrols that had crossed over into Cambodia. In 1974, armed clashes broke out between Vietnamese and Cambodian forces. And in May 1975, barely a month after the Khmer Rouge took power in Kampuchea (their new name for Cambodia), they invaded the Vietnamese island of Phu Quoc, just off the Cambodian coast (Map 2). They also attacked Tho Chu, off the Vietnamese mainland. The Vietnamese Armed Forces quickly recaptured these islands and retaliated by invading the Kampuchean island of Koh Wai. They withdrew from Koh Wai in August of that year.

In April 1977, Khmer forces made incursions into the Vietnamese town of Chau Doc (in An Giang Province), and later in September in what was a prelude to full-scale war, they sent thousands of soldiers into Tay Ninh Province. In response, the Vietnamese sent eight divisions that threw back the attackers. In January 1978, Vietnamese forces entered Kampuchean Svay Rieng Province (Map 2), where they tried to incite the local population to rise up in rebellion against the Khmer government. No uprising occurred, however, forcing the Vietnamese to withdraw from Kampuchea.

Map 2. Vietnamese Invasion of Cambodia. Political unrest in the Indo-China region led to many wars, the most famous being the Vietnam War. In 1978, two communist countries in Indo-China went to war, with Vietnam launching an invasion of Kampuchea (Cambodia).

In January 1978, the Khmer government initiated a purge of suspected disloyal military officers. Consequently, the commanders in Kampuchea's Eastern Military Zone mutinied in protest of the purge. Government forces arrived and quelled the mutiny. Many of the rebelling commanders, accompanied by their military units, escaped to Vietnam where they were welcomed by the government there. The

Vietnamese Army helped re-organize these Kampuchean units into an insurgent movement whose objective was to overthrow the Khmer regime.

In June 1978, Vietnam made preparations to invade Kampuchea. The Vietnamese government wanted to end the Khmer Rouge's cross-border raids into Vietnam that had caused thousands of civilian deaths and great losses in homes and properties. Vietnam also distrusted China's intentions in Indo-China. As China and Kampuchea were allies, Vietnam saw itself surrounded by hostile forces that could invade in the future. The acrimonious Soviet-Chinese relations (that had begun in the 1960s) also fueled tensions, since Vietnam was backed by the Soviet Union, while Kampuchea was supported by China.

By November 1978, Vietnam was massing its forces along its southern border with Kampuchea. Vietnam had taken the precaution of securing its northern region against a possible Chinese invasion by signing the Vietnamese-Soviet Treaty of Friendship and Cooperation, which guaranteed Russian military intervention in case of a Chinese attack.

To counter the Vietnamese military build-up, Kampuchea strengthened its eastern border with 14 Army divisions. Khmer forces were equipped with Chinese weapons, which had begun to arrive in Kampuchea in large quantities.

Following a diversionary attack on Kratie (Map 2), 13 Vietnamese Army divisions, supported by artillery and air cover, advanced through the Kampuchean border in the direction of Phnom Penh. The Khmer forces engaged using conventional warfare but were quickly cut down to pieces by the much stronger Vietnamese Army. Vietnamese battle tanks now raced down the highways toward Phnom Penh, reaching the capital on January 7, 1979. Pol Pot and other high-ranking government officials fled to the western region of Cambodia near the border with Thailand, where they set up a resistance government. In Phnom Penh, a new government was formed, mainly composed of former Khmer Eastern Military Zone exiles, and backed by Vietnam.

The one-sidedness of the war revealed the stark contrast between the steely resolve of the Vietnamese who had just undergone many decades of wars with France and the United States, against the relatively untested Kampuchean Army. Furthermore, the disparity in military strength was significant: Vietnam's Armed Forces included over 600,000 soldiers, 900 tanks, and 300 aircraft, while Kampuchea's forces consisted only of 70,000 soldiers, and a few tanks and aircraft. Another crucial factor was the Khmer Rouge's brutal repression of its people, which saw millions perish from executions, tortures, forced labor, starvation, and diseases, which made the Kampucheans physically, emotionally, and mentally exhausted, and unable to oppose the Vietnamese invasion.

CHINESE CIVIL WAR

In 1911, two thousand years of dynastic imperial rule ended in China. Suddenly left without a central government, the country fragmented into many semi-independent regions. Then from southern China, a political party called the Kuomintang (English: Chinese Nationalist Party) formed a government whose aim was to reunite the country.

The Kuomintang built an army and then began a military campaign for China's reunification, an event known as the Chinese Civil War. The civil war lasted 23 years and consisted of four phases: first, the Kuomintang's defeat of the regional military leaders called warlords; second, the Kuomintang's contentious split into two rival factions, i.e. the right-wing Nationalists and the left-wing and Communists alliance; third, these two rival factions' brief alliance to fight the Japanese who had invaded China; and fourth, the ultimate reunification of China by the victorious Communists in 1950.

Background The origin of the Chinese Civil War can be traced to the early 1900s, with many factors coming into play. Among these factors were the growing opposition of the Han people (China's main ethnic group) to the ruling Qing monarchy; the assimilation of Western political ideas into Chinese thought; China's military defeats to and occupation by the foreign powers; and the country's backwardness in stark contrast to the prosperity and development in the West. These factors shattered the Chinese people's confidence in their government.

In 1911, revolts and civil unrest broke out in many areas of southern China. Being unable to stop the disturbances, the Qing monarchy abdicated, which ended two millennia of Chinese dynastic rule. China was left suddenly without a central government.

In southern China, the Kuomintang emerged and formed a government, and declared that the country was henceforth a republic. Sun Yat-sen, the Kuomintang's leader, became president of China – nominally at least. For in reality, the country had fractured into many semi-autonomous regions after the Qing monarchy's collapse. Sun's first task was to reunify the country under his government through the use of force. However, he lacked an army to carry out a campaign of conquest, especially in the northern region of China where the Qing monarchy still held strong influence. Sun therefore entered into an agreement with Yuan Shikai, the powerful northern military commander, whereby Yuan would cease his support for the Qing monarchy in exchange for Sun stepping down and allowing Yuan to become China's president.

After becoming president, however, Yuan suppressed the Kuomintang and gave himself unlimited powers. He appointed military governors, commonly called warlords, in the provinces, where they held great power and commanded a local army. Warlordism would dominate China's regional politics for many years. With Yuan's death in 1916, China again was left without a central government. The country fragmented into many quasi-independent regions, with each region coming under the control of a warlord.

Sun returned to China, having fled into exile during Yuan's dictatorship. Sun restored the Kuomintang and restarted his plan to reunify the country. This time, however, he decided to build his own army. He turned to the Western powers for military assistance but was turned down. Sun then approached the Soviet Union, which promised him support on the condition that Sun allowed members of the fledging Communist Party of China to join the Kuomintang. Sun agreed.

In 1923, with Soviet funds, Sun founded a military academy to train military recruits for his new army. The recruits came from different ideological backgrounds: Chinese traditionalists, right-wingers, left-wingers, Communists, etc. Thus, the Kuomintang Army that ultimately was formed included many political persuasions.

In 1936, Sun passed away. The Kuomintang was wracked by a power struggle, which ultimately split the party into two factions: the left-wingers (including the small group of Communists) led by Wang Jingwei, who was appointed chairman of the Kuomintang, and therefore Sun's legal successor, and the right-wingers led by General Chiang Kai-shek who, as the commander of the Kuomintang Army, held the real power. Initially, the two sides worked together.

War By July 1927, the Kuomintang Army was built up and ready to go to war. The Kuomintang opened its military campaign along three fronts: the left-wing/Communist faction advanced westward toward Wuhan; a right-wing force headed east for Shanghai; and Chiang's forces, at the center, advanced for Nanjing. Ultimately, the three fronts achieved their military objectives. Within six months, the Kuomintang had defeated 34 warlords along its path towards the central regions of China.

In Nanjing, Chiang began a violent purge of Communist elements of the Kuomintang. During his military training in the Soviet Union, Chiang had determined that Communism, as well as democratic and other Western political ideologies were inapplicable to China. Chiang was a social conservative who believed that Communism was incompatible with China's traditional values. His desire to eliminate Communism reached the intensity of an obsession.

Chiang began his purge in Shanghai where his soldiers killed thousands of unsuspecting Communist civilians who had filled the streets to welcome the Kuomintang Army's arrival. Other purges soon followed in Canton, Xiamen, Ningbo, Nanjing, Hangzhou, and Changsha, where thousands of Communists also were killed.

The remaining Communists went into hiding, some in urban areas, but the vast majority in the countryside, where they began working with and mobilizing the peasants and villagers. With the purges, the alliance between the Kuomintang and the Communist Party of China ended. The Soviet Union also stopped its support for Chiang.

In August 1927, in response to the purges, the Communists in Nanchang broke out in rebellion. Chiang sent his forces to Nanchang, where they easily quelled the rebellion and forced the Communists to flee to the hinterlands of southern China. Another Communist rebellion in Hunan led by Mao Zedong, then a regional commander, was put down as well. Mao and his supporters were forced to retreat to the Jiangxi countryside. There, they established the Chinese Soviet Republic, a quasi-government that formed subordinate administrative councils called "soviets" in other provinces, including Anhui, Fujian, Guangdong, Henan, Hubei, and Sichuan. Mao's government gained widespread support from the local rural population. Initially, its small militia was limited to conducting hit-and-run guerilla warfare against government forces. By mid-1932, however, Mao's militia, now known as the People's Liberation Army, or colloquially, the Red Army, had grown to 45,000 regulars and 200,000 auxiliaries.

Meanwhile, the left-wing Kuomintang faction, led by Wang Jingwei, established Wuhan as its capital, but the city soon was attacked by a warlord ally of Chiang. Wang's government collapsed, leaving Chiang as the undisputed leader of the Kuomintang.

The Nationalists (as Chiang's army now was called) resumed their campaign toward northern China. In June 1938, they captured Beijing, the capital of China's most powerful warlord, who thereafter pledged allegiance to Chiang. Beijing's capture was significant, as the city was the symbolic and historical seat of authority in China. This achievement legitimized Chiang's government, as it meant the complete – albeit symbolic – reunification of the country. Chiang had achieved reunification through military victories, as well as by making alliances with many warlords scattered throughout northern, central, and southern China.

Soon, Chiang's government became recognized by many countries around the world. From his capital in Nanjing, Chiang began to rebuild China along the modern Western model. However, his efforts would be fraught with difficulties and ultimately not be fulfilled.

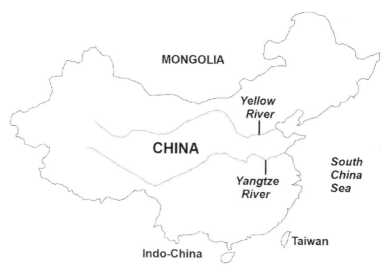

Map 3. China's two major river systems, Yellow River and Yangtze River, served as strategic battle lines between communist and nationalist forces during the latter stages of the Chinese Civil War.

In May 1930, a territorial dispute in China's Central Plains erupted into a major war among regional warlords who had made alliances with the Kuomintang. Soon, Chiang's government was drawn into the war. Over one million soldiers fought in the conflict that claimed high casualty rates on all sides. Ultimately, Chiang succeeded in quelling the rebellion. He realized, however, that China was far from being reunited and that the warlords could pose a constant and serious threat to his authority. Unknown to Chiang at that time, the real danger to his rule would be the Communists.

Soon learning of the existence of Mao's Chinese Soviet Republic, Chiang sent his forces to attack Jiangxi and other Communist-held regions. However, Mao's Communists in Jiangxi were well-entrenched in fortified positions, forcing the Nationalists to mount five military campaigns from 1929 to 1935. Three of these campaigns ended in failures while a fourth was abandoned when the Nationalist forces were redeployed following Japan's invasion of Manchuria in northern China. In the fifth attempt, Chiang's forces changed tactics from a costly frontal attack as in the previous campaigns to a slow, deliberate encirclement and constriction of the enemy positions.

Facing annihilation by the effective Nationalist offensive strategy, Mao and his 80,000 Communist followers were forced to make a breakout and escaped through a weakly defended section in the Nationalists' encirclement. Mao and his followers then began their historic Long March, an 8,000-mile, year-long foot journey toward Yan-an in Shaanxi Province in northern China. Along the way, they endured pursuing Nationalist forces, hostile indigenous tribes, starvation and diseases, and natural barriers that included freezing, snow-covered mountains, raging rivers, and a vast expanse of swampland.

Only 6,000 of Mao's followers survived the journey – less than a tenth of the original number that had set out. Other Communist forces, including two large armies, also escaped the Nationalists' encirclement and embarked on their own journeys through different routes, with all making it to Yan'an. Mao had arrived there first, however, with the most survivors, and had established his authority over the Chinese Communists, which thereafter was not challenged.

On learning that the Communists had escaped to Yan'an, Chiang travelled to northern China in December 1936 to plan his attack against Mao's forces. However, the Nationalist commanders in Yan'an were infuriated that the Japanese had invaded Manchuria and were annexing Chinese territories while fellow Chinese were fighting each other. At gunpoint, the Nationalist commanders forced Chiang to cancel his campaign against the Red Army and agree to a Nationalist-Communist alliance to fight the Japanese.

Map 4. China's provinces that were affected during the Chinese Civil War.

On learning of the alliance, the Japanese forces launched a pre-emptive, full-scale invasion of China in July 1937. They easily captured the coastal cities of China's eastern provinces; the Nationalist strongholds of Shanghai, Nanjing, and Wuhan also fell.

The events during the Japanese invasion turned the tide of the Chinese Civil War away from the Nationalists in favor of the Communists. The major Japanese offensives were conducted along China's coastal, central, and later, with the outbreak of World War II in the Pacific, in the southern regions, all of which were Nationalist-held territories. These offensives inflicted great losses in men and material to the Nationalist forces. In the defense of Shanghai, for example, Chiang lost 200,000 soldiers and his best military commanders.

Chiang also committed major military blunders. At Nanjing, for instance, he allowed his forces to be trapped and then destroyed. Consequently, the Japanese killed 200,000 civilians and soldiers in the city. Then in a scorched earth strategy to delay the enemy's advance, Chiang ordered the dams destroyed around Nanjing, which caused the Yellow River to flood and kill 500,000 people. Furthermore, as the Nationalist forces retreated westward, they set fire to Changsha to prevent the city's capture by the Japanese, but this resulted in the deaths of 20,000 residents and the displacement of hundreds of thousands more, who were not told of the plan.

The Chinese people's confidence in their government plummeted, as it seemed to them that the Nationalist Army was incapable of saving the country. At the same time, the Communists' popularity soared because, unlike the Nationalists who used costly open warfare against the Japanese, the Red Army employed guerilla tactics with great success against the mostly lightly defended enemy outposts in remote areas.

Soon, Chiang realized the futility of resisting the vastly superior Japanese forces. He therefore preferred to retreat instead of committing large numbers of troops into battle. Furthermore, he wanted to conserve his forces for what he believed was the eventual continuation of the war with the Communists. The civilian population was infuriated, however, as they believed that the Japanese were the enemy to be fought and under whom they were undergoing so much suffering.

In reality, the Nationalist-Communist alliance was superficial, for although the two sides fought the Japanese in their respective areas of control, considerable tensions existed between the two rival Chinese forces that sometimes led to the outbreak of skirmishes for control of territories that had not yet fallen to the Japanese. In January 1941, the fragile alliance was broken when the Nationalist forces attacked the Red Army in Anhui and Jiangsu, killing thousands of Communist soldiers.

Corruption was rampant among the high-ranking civilian and military leaders of the Nationalist government. Chiang later cited in his memoirs that his government's corruption was the leading cause for his defeat to the Communists. So severe was the corruption that the United States, which was propping up the Nationalist Army with large amounts of military aid, demanded to take command of Chiang's destitute, ill-fed, and under-equipped soldiers (ostensibly caused by the Nationalist generals' diversion of the money into their own pockets) with the threat of ending American assistance. When Chiang threatened to make peace with Japan, however, the Americans acquiesced and agreed to a compromise. And just as the Nationalists were beset by military defeats and government corruption, the Communists were gaining strength and influence in northern China.

When the Japanese forces withdrew from China following their defeat in World War II, the civil war had shifted invariably in favor of the Communists. The Red Army now constituted 1.2 million soldiers and 2 million armed auxiliaries, with many more millions of civilian volunteers ready to provide logistical support. Mao controlled one quarter of China's territories and one third of the population, all in areas that largely had escaped the destruction of World War II.

By contrast, the Nationalist government had been weakened seriously by World War II. The Nationalists' territories were devastated and were facing huge economic problems. Thousands of people were left homeless and destitute.

Nearing the end of World War II, the Soviet Union launched a major offensive against the Japanese forces in Manchuria, the industrial heartland where Japan manufactured its weapons and military equipment. The Soviets subsequently withdrew from China but not before allowing the Chinese Communists to occupy large sections of Manchuria (up to 97% of the total area) before the Nationalist Army arrived to take the remaining three Manchurian cities, which were geographically separated from each other.

After the Soviets and the Japanese had withdrawn from China after World War II, armed clashes began to break out between the Nationalist and Communist forces. It seemed only a matter of time before full-scale war would follow. In January 1946, the United States mediated a peace agreement between the two sides. However, the Nationalists and Communists continued their arms build-up and war posturing, which eventually led to the breakdown of the truce in June 1946 and the start of the final and decisive phase of the civil war.

In July 1946, Chiang launched a large-scale offensive with 1.6 million soldiers, with the aim of destroying Mao's forces in northern China. Because of their superior weapons, the Nationalists advanced steadily. The Red Army also pulled back as part of its strategy of luring on the Nationalists and then letting them overextend their forward lines. In March 1947, the Nationalists captured Yan'an, the former Communists' headquarters, which really was inconsequential as Mao had moved the bulk of his forces further north.

By September 1948, the Red Army had become much bigger and stronger than the Nationalist forces. Mao finalized plans for a general counter-offensive that ultimately brought the war to an end. From their bases in Manchuria, one million Red Army soldiers swept down over Nationalist-held Shenyang, Changchun, and Jinzhou, encircling these cities and then capturing them. By November 1948, the whole of Manchuria had come under the Communists' control. Five hundred thousand Nationalist soldiers had been killed, wounded, or captured.

The Red Army continued its offensive to the south and took Beijing and Tianjin following heavy fighting. After incurring losses totaling some 200,000 soldiers, the remaining 260,000 Nationalist defenders in Beijing surrendered to the Communists. By late January 1949, the Communists held all of northern China.

A few weeks before the Beijing campaign, another Red Army offensive consisting of 800,000 soldiers and 600,000 auxiliaries descended on Xuzhou. By mid-January 1949, the Communists had gained control of the Provinces of Shandong, Jiangsu, Anhui, and Henan – and all the territories north of the Yangtze River. More than five million peasants volunteered as laborers for the Red Army, reflecting the Communists' massive support in the rural areas. Furthermore, many leading Nationalist Army officers had begun to defect to the Communists. The defectors handed the Red Army vital military information, seriously compromising the Nationalists' war effort.

After the Nationalist Army's crushing defeats in northern and central China, the war essentially was over. Chiang's remaining forces were hard pressed to mount further effective resistance against the Red Army's offensives. Starting with their injudicious offensive in 1946, the Nationalists had lost 1.5 million soldiers, including their best military units. Vast amounts of Nationalist stockpiles of weapons and military hardware had fallen to the Red Army.

Map 5. China's cities that were affected during the Chinese Civil War. Nationalist forces under Chiang Kai-shek retreated to the island of Taiwan (lower right) after their defeat in the war.

With ever-growing numbers of troops and weapons, Communist forces made their final advance south virtually unopposed toward the remaining Nationalist territories in southern and southwestern China. At this time, the United States ended its military support to the Nationalist government. Chiang moved China's national art treasures and vast quantities of gold and foreign-currency reserves from the National Treasury to the island of Taiwan, causing great uproar among high-ranking officials in his government.

After unsuccessful attempts to negotiate the surrender of the Nationalist government, the Red Army crossed the Yangtze River and captured Nanjing, the former capital of the Nationalists, who meanwhile had moved their headquarters to Guangdong Province.

A disagreement arose among Nationalist leaders whether to defend all remaining territories still under their control or to pull back to a smaller but more defensible area. By October 1949, the Red Army had broken through Guangdong, but not before the Nationalists moved their capital to Chongqing.

On October 1, 1949, Mao declared the establishment of the People's Republic of China. On December 10, 1949, as Red Army forces were encircling Chengdu, the last Nationalist stronghold, Chiang departed on a plane for Taiwan. Joining him in Taiwan were about two million Chinese mainlanders, mostly Kuomintang officials, Nationalist Army officers and soldiers, prominent members of society, the academe, and the religious orders. On March 1, 1950, Chiang resumed his position as China's president and declared Taiwan as the temporary capital of the Republic of China.

In the months that followed, fighting continued to flare up between the military forces of the two Chinese governments, mainly for possession of the islands along the waters separating their countries. Since no truce or peace agreement was made by and between the two governments that do not recognize the legitimacy of the other, to this day, the two countries are technically still at war.

LANDING OPERATION ON HAINAN ISLAND

Background After its defeat in the Chinese Civil War *(previous article)*, the Nationalist government, now based in Taiwan, still held Hainan, an island located just 16 kilometers off the Chinese mainland (Map 6). At its nearest point, the island is only nine kilometers from the mainland, with all but two kilometers of a shallow depth that can be waded ashore by invading troops. Hainan is of moderate size, being 155 kilometers long and 170 kilometers wide.

The Nationalists, believing that it was just a matter of time before the Communists would try to seize the island, strengthened Hainan's defenses by sending more troops to guard strategic points all along the coast. Navy ships and some warplanes were also sent to the island.

Under utmost secrecy, Red China made detailed preparations for an amphibious invasion of Hainan. The invasion called for the use of 2,000 junks (Chinese moderate-size wooden water vessels) to transport and land several thousands of soldiers. (At that time, China lacked a navy, since the Nationalists had moved the whole Chinese Navy fleet to Taiwan.) Preparatory to the invasion, covert small-scale landings were to be made on specified points on Hainan's northwestern and northeastern shores, to be followed by two waves of the main invasion force landing directly on the northern coast. All three landings would then converge on the north and destroy Hainan's main garrison.

Invasion In late March 1950, under cover of evening darkness, 800 Communist soldiers landed in Chaotouxu in Hainan's northwest coast. A few days later, 3,000 soldiers landed in Chisui in the island's northeast shore. The landings were aided by the island's 17,000 communist civilians who provided the landing points, and reconnaissance information regarding the island's defenses. The newly arrived troops soon were joined by Red Army squads that had landed in the island earlier that year.

On the night of April 10, 1950, the first wave of the Red Chinese main invasion force, consisting of 12,000 soldiers aboard 350 motorized junks, set out from the Leizhou Peninsula in southern China. While the junks were crossing Hainan Strait, they were spotted by Nationalist Navy ships, which moved in to attack. Another flotilla of Communist junks, however, moved into position behind the Nationalist ships. A naval battle followed. The Communists fired at the Nationalist ships using field guns retrofitted on the junks. The artillery fire from the Nationalist ships was ineffective, as their rounds, intended for armor, simply smashed into the wooden junks without detonating. Following several hours of fighting, the Nationalist ships withdrew after sustaining heavy damage. Foggy conditions during the night prevented the Nationalist warplanes from joining the battle.

The first wave of the Communists' main invasion force landed along two points located north of the island. These assaults were aided by Communist soldiers from the earlier landings who had advanced north to attack the other Nationalist garrisons. On April 17, 1950, the main Nationalist garrison on the island collapsed, allowing more Communist troops to pour into Hainan.

After establishing a beachhead, the invading forces launched a three-pronged offensive to the south: one toward the southeast, another along the west, and the third through the interior. By May 1, the whole island had been captured. One hundred thousand Nationalist soldiers were taken prisoner; some 60,000 escaped by sea and air to Taiwan.

The Nationalists' defeat in Hainan sent shock waves all across Taiwan where desperation began to set in among the civilian population. The United States, having ceased support for President Chiang Kai-shek's government, believed that Taiwan would fall before the end of 1950.

Map 6. Hainan Island in southern China. In April 1950, Chinese communist forces from the Leizhou Peninsula crossed Hainan Strait and invaded Hainan. After three weeks of fighting, Nationalist forces defending the island were defeated.

Encouraged by the success of the Hainan invasion, China began preparations to invade Taiwan. Tens of thousands of Red Army soldiers were assembled, as were thousands of fishermen who were enlisted to pilot the thousands of junks needed for the operation. Commercial freighters were retrofitted for naval combat and sunken warships from the Chinese Civil War were raised and repaired.

The planned Chinese invasion of Taiwan, however, did not materialize. In June 1950, North Korea invaded South Korea, where U.S. Army troops were stationed. Suddenly dragged into the conflict now known as the Korean War, the United States broke its neutrality in the region and sent its Seventh Naval Fleet into the Korean Peninsula. The U.S. naval presence and renewed American support for Chiang's government forced China to cancel its planned invasion of Taiwan.

ANGLO-AFGHAN WAR OF 1919

During the early years of the twentieth century, Tsarist Russia and the British Empire in India were the regional powers in Central Asia. The devastating effects of World War I on these two regional powers had a profound effect on the Anglo-Afghan War of 1919. In Russia, the Tsarist government had collapsed and a bitter civil war was raging. Consequently, Russia's control of its Central Asian domains was weakened. The British Empire, which included the Indian subcontinent (Map 7), was drained financially and militarily, despite emerging victorious in World War I.

With the two regional powers weakened by war, the semi-independent Emirate of Afghanistan moved to assert its right of sovereignty. More important, Habibullah, the Afghan ruler, wanted to annul the Treaty of Gandamak, where Afghanistan had ceded its foreign policy decisions to the British Empire. Adding strength to Habibullah's diplomatic position was that he had allowed Afghanistan to stay neutral during World War I, despite the strong anti-British sentiments among his people. Habibullah had also spurned Germany and the Ottoman Empire, enemies of the British, who had encouraged him to defy British domination in the region and even launch an attack on British India, at a time when Britain was most vulnerable.

For these reasons, Habibullah asked the British to allow him to present his case for Afghanistan's independence at the Paris Peace Conference, where the victorious Allied countries had gathered to discuss the end of World War I. Habibullah was assassinated, however, before his case was decided. His son, Amanullah, succeeded to the Afghan throne, despite a rival claim by a family relative.

Upon his ascent to the throne, Amanullah declared Afghanistan's independence, doing away with his father's policy of trying to gain the country's sovereignty through diplomatic means. The declaration of independence was immensely popular among Afghans, as nationalist sentiments ran high. Amanullah therefore was able to consolidate his hold on power, even as some sectors opposed his leadership. Amanullah provoked the British by inciting an uprising of the tribal people in Peshawar, British India. Using the uprising as a diversion, he sent his forces across the Afghan-British Indian border to capture the town of Bagh.

The British Army quickly quelled the Peshawar uprising and threw back the Afghan forces across the border. The Afghans clearly were unprepared for war – although having sufficient numbers of soldiers as well as being assisted by tribal militias, they possessed obsolete weapons, which even then were in short supply.

By contrast, the British were a modern fighting machine because of the technological advances they had made in World War I. The British suffered from a shortage of soldiers, since much of their forces had yet to return to India from their deployment to other British territories during World War I. The British air attacks on Kabul devastated Afghan morale, forcing Amanullah to sue for peace.

Afghanistan and the British Empire entered into peace negotiations to end the war. In the peace treaty that emerged from these negotiations, the British granted conciliatory terms to the Afghans, including returning Afghanistan's right of foreign policy. The British, therefore, essentially recognized Afghanistan as a sovereign state. By this time, Afghanistan already had been nominally independent, as it had established diplomatic relations with the newly formed Soviet Union and its independence was gaining recognition by the international community.

Afghanistan and the British Empire retained the Durand Line as their common border. After the war, Afghanistan continued to serve as a buffer zone between the Russians and the British, because of the end of the previous non-aggression treaties between Tsarist Russia and the British Empire following the emergence of the Soviet Union after the Russian Civil War.

Map 7. Anglo-Afghan War of 1919. The British Empire's prized possession during the nineteenth and twentieth centuries was the Indian subcontinent. Afghanistan served as a neutral zone between the region's two major powers, the Russian Empire and the British Empire.

1947-1948 CIVIL WAR IN PALESTINE

Background Through a League of Nations mandate, Britain administered Palestine from 1920 to 1948. For nearly all that time, the British rule was plagued by violence between the rival Arabs and Jewish populations that resided in Palestine. The Palestinian Arabs resented the British for allowing the Jews to settle in what the Arabs believed was their ancestral land. The Palestinian Jews also were hostile to the British for limiting and sometimes even preventing other Jews from entering Palestine. The Jews believed that Palestine had been promised to them as the site of their future nation. Arabs and Jews clashed against each other; they also attacked the British authorities. Bombings, massacres, assassinations, and other violent civilian incidents occurred frequently in Palestine.

By the end of World War II in 1945, nationalist aspirations had risen among the Palestinian Arabs and Palestinian Jews. Initially, Britain proposed an independent Palestine consisting of federated states of Arabs and Jews, but later deemed the plan unworkable because of the uninterrupted violence. The British, therefore, referred the issue of Palestine to the United Nations (UN). The British also announced their intention to give up their mandate over Palestine, end all administrative functions there, and withdraw their troops by May 15, 1948. The last British troops actually left on June 30, 1948.

The UN offered a proposal for the partition for Palestine (Map 8) which the UN General Assembly subsequently approved on November 29, 1947. The Palestinian Jews accepted the plan, whereas the Palestinian Arabs rejected it. The Palestinian Arabs took issue with what they felt was the unfair division of Palestine in relation to the Arab-Jewish population ratio. The Jews made up 32% of Palestine's population but would acquire 56% of the land. The Arabs, who comprised 68% of the population, would gain 43% of Palestine. The lands proposed for the Jews, however, had a mixed population composed of 46% Arabs and 54% Jews. The areas of Palestine allocated to the Arabs consisted of 99% Arabs and 1% Jews. No population transfer was proposed. Jerusalem and its surrounding areas, with their mixed population of 100,000 Jews and an equal number of Arabs, were to be administered by the UN.

War Shortly after the UN approved the partition plan, hostilities broke out in Palestine. Armed bands of Jews and Arabs attacked rival villages and settlements, threw explosives into crowded streets, and ambushed or used land mines against vehicles plying the roads. Attacks and punitive attacks occurred; single gunfire shots led to widespread armed clashes.

By the end of May 1948, over 2,000 Palestinian civilians (Arabs and Jews) had been killed and thousands more had been wounded. The British still held legal authority over Palestine, but did little to stop the violence, as they were in the process of withdrawing their forces and disengaging from further involvement in the region's internal affairs. The British did interfere in a few instances and suffered casualties as well.

A large Jewish paramilitary, as well as a number of smaller Jewish militias, already existed and operated clandestinely during the period of the British mandate. As the violence escalated, Jewish leaders integrated these armed groups into a single Jewish Army.

Fighting on the side of the Palestinian Arabs were two rival armed groups: a smaller militia composed of Palestinian Arab fighters, and a larger paramilitary organized by the neighboring Arab countries.

Egypt, Syria, and Jordan did not want to send their armies to Palestine at this time since this would be an act of war against powerful Britain.

During the course of the war, the Jews experienced major logistical problems with the distant Jewish settlements that were separated from the main Jewish strongholds along the coast. These Jewish exclaves included Jerusalem, where one-sixth of all Palestinian Jews lived, as well as the many small villages and settlements in the north (Galilee) and in the south (Negev).

Jewish leaders sent militia units to these areas to augment existing local defense forces that consisted solely of local civilians. These isolated settlements were instructed to hold their ground at all costs. Supplying these Jewish exclaves was particularly dangerous, as delivery convoys were ambushed and had to traverse many Arab settlements along the way. Food rationing, therefore, was imposed in many distant Jewish settlements, a policy that persisted until the war's end.

The Jews gained a clear advantage in the fighting after they had organized a unified army. Their military leaders imposed mandatory conscription of men and single women, first only for the younger adult age groups, and later, for all men under age 40 and single women up to age 35. By April 1948, the Jewish Army had numbered 21,000 soldiers, up significantly from the few thousands at the start of the war.

The Jews also increased their weapons stockpiles from generous contributions made by wealthy donors in Europe and the United States. As the UN had imposed an arms embargo on Palestine, the Jews smuggled in their weapons, which were purchased mainly from dealers in Czechoslovakia. These weapons began to arrive in Palestine early in the fighting, greatly enhancing the Jews' war effort. The Jews also procured some weapons from clandestine small-arms manufacturers in Palestine; however, the output from local manufacturers was insufficient to fill the demands of the Jews' growing army as well as the widening conflict.

Starting in April 1948, the Jewish Army launched a number of offensives aimed at securing Jewish territories as well as protecting Jewish civilians in Arab-held areas. These Jewish operations were carried out in anticipation of the Arab armies intervening in Palestine once the British Mandate ended on May 15, 1948.

On April 2, 1948, Jewish forces advanced toward Jerusalem in order to lift the siege on the city and allow the entry of supply vehicles. The Jews cleared the roads of Arab fighters and took control of the Arab villages nearby. The operation was only partially successful, however, as Jewish delivery convoys continued to be ambushed along the roads. Furthermore, Jewish authorities were condemned by the international community after a Jewish attack on the Arab village of Deir Yassin resulted in the deaths of over one hundred Arab civilians.

On April 8, Jewish forces succeeded in lifting the siege on Mishmar Haemek, a Jewish kibbutz in the Jezreel Valley. The Jews then launched a counter-attack that captured nearby Arab settlements. Further offensives allowed the Jews to seize control of northeastern Palestine. Also falling to Jewish forces were Tiberias in mid-April, Haifa and Jaffa later in the month, and Beisan and Safed in May. In southern Palestine, the Jews captured key areas in the Negev. The Jewish offensives greatly reduced the Palestinian Arabs' capacity to continue the war.

In the wake of the Jewish victories, hundreds of thousands of Arab civilians fled from their homes, leaving scores of empty villages that were looted and destroyed by Jewish forces. Earlier in 1948, tens of thousands of middle-class and upper-class Arabs had left Palestine for safety in neighboring Arab countries. Jewish authorities formally annexed captured Arab lands, merging them with Jewish territories already under their control.

On May 14, 1948, one day before the end of the British Mandate in Palestine, the Jews declared independence as the State of Israel. The following day, British rule in Palestine ended. Within a few hours, the armies of the Arab countries, specifically those from Egypt, Jordan, Syria, Lebanon, and Iraq, invaded the new country of Israel, triggering the second phase of the conflict – the 1948 Arab-Israeli War *(next article)*.

Map 8. United Nations Partition Plan for Palestine. The original plan released by the UN proposed to allocate 56% of Palestine to Jews, while 43% would be allotted to Palestinian Arabs. Jerusalem, at 1% of the territory, would be administered by the UN (map redrawn after Morris, 2008).

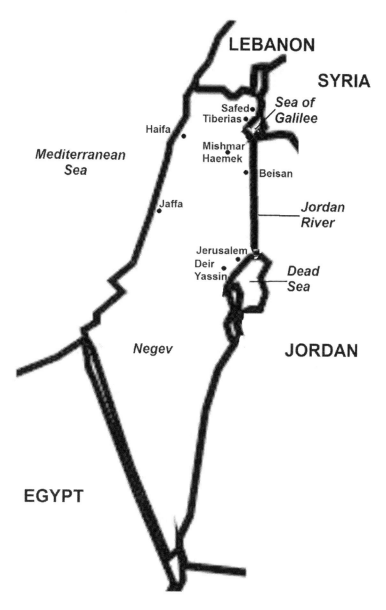

Map 9. 1947-1948 Civil War in Palestine. Some key battle areas are shown.

1948 ARAB-ISRAELI WAR

On May 14, 1948, the Palestinian Jews established the State of Israel. The next day, the infant nation was attacked by the armies of Egypt, Jordan, Syria, Lebanon, and Iraq, assisted by volunteer fighters from other Arab states. The Arabs' stated reasons for the invasion were to stop the violence and to restore law and order in Palestine, and to allow the Palestinian people to form a government of their choice. Also cited by the Arabs was the displacement of Palestinian Arabs caused by Jewish aggression. As the nation of Israel was by now in existence, the resulting 1948 Arab-Israeli War was one fought by sovereign states.

From the east, Jordanian and Iraqi forces crossed the Jordan River into Palestine. The Jordanians advanced along two columns for Jerusalem, which they surrounded on May 17, 1948. After heavy house-to-house fighting, the Jewish defenders of the city were forced to surrender when they ran low on food and ammunition. The Jordanians captured Jerusalem and then occupied Latrun, a strategic outpost overlooking the highway that led to Jerusalem.

Meanwhile, the Iraqis advanced to the vicinity surrounding the Arab-populated city of Jenin, Nablus, and Tulkaran. On May 25, they captured Geulim, Kfar Vona, and Ein Vered before being stopped at Natanya, their ultimate objective on the western coast. Natanya's fall would have divided Israel's coastal areas in two.

A strong Israeli counterattack on Jenin forced the Iraqis to pull back and defend the city. The Iraqis repulsed the Israeli attack. Now, however, they were concerned with making further advances because of the risk of being cut off from the rear. The Iraqis, therefore, switched to a defensive position, which they maintained for the rest of the war.

From the northeast, Syrian forces began their campaign by advancing toward the south side of the Sea of Galilee. They captured some Israeli villages before being defeated at Degania. The Syrians soon withdrew across the border in order to regroup. On June 6, they launched another attack, this time in northern Galilee, where they captured Mishmar Hayarden. Israeli Army reinforcements soon arrived in northern Palestine, stopping further Syrian advances.

From the south, the Egyptian Army, which was the largest among the invading forces, entered Palestine through the Sinai Desert. The Egyptians then advanced through southern Palestine on two fronts: one along the coastal road for Tel-Aviv, and another through the central Negev for Jerusalem.

On June 11, 1948, the United Nations (UN) imposed a truce, which lasted for 28 days until July 8. A UN panel arrived in Palestine to work out a deal among the warring sides. The UN effort, however, failed to bring about a peace agreement.

By the end of the first weeks of the war, the Israeli Army had stopped the supposed Arab juggernaut that the Israelis had feared would simply roll in and annihilate their fledging nation. Although the fighting essentially had ended in a stalemate, Israeli morale was bolstered considerably, as many Israeli villages had been saved by sheer determination alone. Local militias had thrown back entire Arab regular army units.

Earlier on May 26, Israeli authorities had merged the various small militias and a large Jewish paramilitary into a single Israeli Defense Force, the country's regular armed forces. Mandatory conscription into the military service was imposed, enabling Israel to double the size of its forces from 30,000 to 60,000 soldiers. Despite the UN arms embargo, the Israeli government was able to purchase large quantities of weapons and military equipment, including heavy firearms, artillery pieces, battle tanks, and warplanes.

The Arabs were handicapped seriously by the UN arms restriction, as the Western countries that supplied much of the Arabs' weapons adhered to the embargo. Consequently, Arab soldiers experienced ammunition shortages during the fighting, forcing the Arab armies to switch from offensive to defensive positions. Furthermore, Arab reinforcements simply could not match in numbers, zeal, and determination the new Israeli conscripts arriving at the front lines. And just as important, the war revealed the efficiency, preparedness, and motivation of the Israeli Army in stark contrast to the inefficiency, disunity, and inexperience of the Arab forces.

During the truce, the UN offered a new partition plan, which was rejected by the warring sides. Fighting restarted on July 8, one day before the end of the truce. On July 9, Israeli Army units in the center launched an offensive aimed at opening a corridor from Tel-Aviv to eastern Palestine, in order to lift the siege on Jerusalem. The Israelis captured Lydda and Ramle, two Arab strongholds near Tel-Aviv, forcing thousands of Arab civilians to flee from their homes to escape the fighting. The Israelis reached Latrun, just outside Jerusalem, where they failed to break the solid Jordanian defenses, despite making repeated assaults using battle tanks and heavy armored vehicles. The Israelis also failed to break into the Old City of Jerusalem, and eventually were forced to withdraw.

On July 16, however, a powerful Israeli offensive in northern Palestine captured Nazareth and the whole region of lower Galilee extending from Haifa in the coastal west to the Sea of Galilee in the east. Further north, the Syrian Army continued to hold Mishmar Hayarden after stopping an Israeli attempt to take the town.

In southern Palestine, the Egyptian offensives in Negba (July 12), Gal (July 14), and Be-erot Yitzhak were thrown back by the Israeli Army, with disproportionately high Egyptian casualties. On July 18, the UN imposed a second truce, this time of no specified duration.

The truce lasted nearly three months, when on October 15, fighting broke out once more. During the truce, relative calm prevailed in Palestine despite high tensions and the occasional outbreaks of small-scale fighting. The UN also proposed new changes to the partition plan which, however, were rejected once more by the warring sides.

Map 10. 1948 Arab-Israeli War. Key battle areas are shown. The Arab countries of Egypt, Jordan, Syria, Lebanon, and Iraq, assisted by volunteer fighters from other Arab states, invaded newly formed Israel that had occupied a sizable portion of Palestine.

On September 22, the Israeli government passed a law that made all captured territories an integral part of Israel, including those that would be won in the future. By the autumn of 1948, the Israeli Army totaled 90,000 soldiers, greatly outnumbering the combined Arab expeditionary forces. Large shipments of war materials continued to arrive in Israel.

In mid-October 1948, Israeli forces attacked and captured Egyptian-held Beersheba and Bayt Jibrin. Consequently, the whole Negev came under Israeli control, with 4,000 Egyptian troops trapped in al-Faluja and Iraq al-Manshiyya, two villages near Ashkelon. Israeli warships blocked the Egyptian Navy from rescuing the trapped soldiers.

Later in October, the UN imposed a third truce. Fighting, however, continued in Marmon in northern Palestine. On October 24, another powerful Israeli offensive captured the whole northern Galilee, forcing Syrian and Lebanese Army units, including Arab paramilitary auxiliaries, to withdraw across their respective borders. Tens of thousands of Palestinian civilians fled or were forced to leave to escape the fighting, although many other Arab residents (about 20%) remained. Those who remained eventually were granted Israeli citizenship.

In early November 1948, Israeli forces pursuing Lebanese troops into the border penetrated five miles into Lebanon and captured many Lebanese villages. Israel later withdrew its forces from Lebanon after both countries signed an armistice at the end of the war.

On December 22, Israeli forces attacked Egyptian Army units positioned in the southern Negev, driving them across the Egyptian border after five days of fighting. The Israelis then crossed into the Sinai Peninsula and advanced toward al-Arish to trap the Egyptian

Army. Britain and the United States exerted pressure on Israel, forcing the latter to withdraw its forces from the Sinai.

Map 11. The 1948 Arab-Israeli War. Palestine and adjacent countries are shown, as are the West Bank and the Gaza Strip.

On January 3, 1949, the Israeli Army surrounded the Egyptian forces inside the Gaza Strip in southwestern Palestine. Three days later, Egypt agreed to a ceasefire, which soon came into effect. The 1948 Arab-Israeli War was over. In the following months, Israel signed separate armistices with Egypt, Lebanon, Jordan and Syria.

At war's end, Israel held 78% of Palestine, 22% more than was allotted to the Jews in the original UN partition plan. Israel's territories comprised the whole Galilee and Jezreel Valley in the north, the whole Negev in the south, the coastal plains, and West Jerusalem. Jordan acquired the West Bank, while Egypt gained the Gaza Strip. No Palestinian Arab state was formed.

During the 1948 Arab-Israeli War, and the 1947-1948 Civil War in Palestine *(previous article)* that preceded it, over 700,000 Palestinian Arabs fled from their homes, with most of them eventually settling in the West Bank, Gaza Strip, and southern Lebanon (Map 11). About 10,000 Palestinian Jews also were displaced by the conflict. Furthermore, as a consequence of these wars, tens of thousands of Jews left or were forced to leave from many Arab countries. Most of these Jewish refugees settled in Israel.

BOSNIAN WAR

Background Bosnia-Herzegovina has three main ethnic groups: Bosniaks (Bosnian Muslims), comprising 44% of the population, Bosnian Serbs, with 32%, and Bosnian Croats, with 17%. Slovenia and Croatia declared their independences in June 1991. On October 15, 1991, the Bosnian parliament declared the independence of Bosnia-Herzegovina, with Bosnian Serb delegates boycotting the session in protest. Then acting on a request from both the Bosnian parliament and the Bosnian Serb leadership, a European Economic Community arbitration commission gave its opinion, on January 11, 1992, that Bosnia-Herzegovina's independence cannot be recognized, since no referendum on independence had taken place.

Bosnian Serbs formed a majority in Bosnia's northern regions. On January 5, 1992, Bosnian Serbs seceded from Bosnia-Herzegovina and established their own country. Bosnian Croats, who also comprised a sizable minority, had earlier (on November 18, 1991) seceded from Bosnia-Herzegovina by declaring their own independence. Bosnia-Herzegovina, therefore, fragmented into three republics, formed along ethnic lines.

Furthermore, in March 1991, Serbia and Croatia, two Yugoslav constituent republics located on either side of Bosnia-Herzegovina, secretly agreed to annex portions of Bosnia-Herzegovina that contained a majority population of ethnic Serbians and ethnic Croatians. This agreement, later re-affirmed by Serbians and Croatians in a second meeting in May 1992, was intended to avoid armed conflict between them. By this time, heightened tensions among the three ethnic groups were leading to open hostilities.

Mediators from Britain and Portugal made a final attempt to avert war, eventually succeeding in convincing Bosniaks, Bosnian Serbs, and Bosnian Croats to agree to share political power in a decentralized government. Just ten days later, however, the Bosnian government reversed its decision and rejected the agreement after taking issue with some of its provisions.

War At any rate, by March 1992, fighting had already broken out when Bosnian Serb forces attacked Bosniak villages in eastern Bosnia. Of the three sides, Bosnian Serbs were the most powerful early in the war, as they were backed by the Yugoslav Army. At their peak, Bosnian Serbs had 150,000 soldiers, 700 tanks, 700 armored personnel carriers, 3,000 artillery pieces, and several aircraft. Many Serbian militias also joined the Bosnian Serb regular forces.

Bosnian Croats, with the support of Croatia, had 150,000 soldiers and 300 tanks. Bosniaks were at a great disadvantage, however, as they were unprepared for war. Although much of Yugoslavia's war arsenal was stockpiled in Bosnia-Herzegovina, the weapons were held by the Yugoslav Army (which became the Bosnian Serbs' main fighting force in the early stages of the war). A United Nations (UN) arms embargo on Yugoslavia was devastating to Bosniaks, as they were prohibited from purchasing weapons from foreign sources.

In March and April 1992, the Yugoslav Army and Bosnian Serb forces launched large-scale operations in eastern and northwest Bosnia-Herzegovina. These offensives were so powerful that large sections of Bosniak and Bosnian Croat territories were captured and came under Bosnian Serb control. By the end of 1992, Bosnian Serbs controlled 70% of Bosnia-Herzegovina.

Then under a UN-imposed resolution, the Yugoslav Army was ordered to leave Bosnia-Herzegovina. However, the Yugoslav Army's withdrawal did not affect seriously the Bosnian Serbs' military capability, as a great majority of the Yugoslav soldiers in Bosnia-Herzegovina were ethnic Serbs. These soldiers simply joined the ranks of the Bosnian Serb forces and continued fighting, using the same weapons and ammunitions left over by the departing Yugoslav Army.

In mid-1992, a UN force arrived in Bosnia-Herzegovina that was tasked to protect civilians and refugees and to provide humanitarian aid. Fighting between Bosniaks and Bosnian Croats occurred in Herzegovina (the southern regions) and central Bosnia, mostly in areas where Bosnian Muslims formed a civilian majority. Bosnian Croat forces held the initiative, conducting offensives in Novi Travnik and Prozor. Intense artillery shelling reduced Gornji Vakuf to rubble; surrounding Bosniak villages also were taken, resulting in many civilian casualties.

In May 1992, the Lasva Valley came under attack from the Bosnian Croat forces who, for 11 months, subjected the region to intense artillery shelling and ground attacks that claimed the lives of 2,000 mostly civilian casualties. The city of Mostar, divided into Muslim and Croat sectors, was the scene of bitter fighting, heavy artillery bombardment, and widespread destruction that resulted in thousands of civilian deaths. Numerous atrocities were committed in Mostar.

By July 1993, however, Bosniaks had formed a relatively competent military force that was armed with weapons produced from a rapidly growing local arms-manufacturing industry. Bosniaks, therefore, were better able to defend their territories, and even launch some of their own limited offensive operations.

Then in early 1994, with another Bosnian Serb general offensive looming, Bosniaks and Bosnian Croats found common ground. With the urging of the United States, on February 23, 1994, Bosniaks and Bosnian Croats formed a unified government under the "Federation of

Bosnia and Herzegovina". The civil war shifted to fighting between the combined Bosniak-Bosnian Croat forces against the Bosnian Serb Army.

In early 1994, Bosnian Serb forces laid siege to Sarajevo, Bosnia's capital, relentlessly pounding the city with heavy artillery and inflicting heavy civilian casualties. The siege of the capital drew international condemnation, with the UN and the North Atlantic Treaty Organization (NATO) becoming increasingly involved in the war. NATO declared Bosnia-Herzegovina a no-fly zone. On February 28, 1994, NATO warplanes downed four Serbian aircraft over Banja Luka.

Under a UN threat of a NATO airstrike, Bosnian Serbs were forced to lift the siege on Maglaj; supply convoys thus were able to reach the city by land, the first time in nearly ten months. In April 1994, NATO warplanes attacked Bosnian Serb forces that were threatening a UN-protected area in Gorazde. Later that month, a Danish contingent of the UN forces engaged Bosnian Serb Army units in the village of Kalesija. The NATO air strikes, which greatly contributed to ending the war, were conducted in coordination with the UN humanitarian and peacekeeping forces in Bosnia-Herzegovina.

With the US lifting its arms embargo on Bosnia-Herzegovina in November 1994, Bosniak forces began to receive shipments of American weapons. The UN was also alarmed at the increasing reports of atrocities being committed by Bosnian Serb forces. After Bosnian Serb artillery attacks killed 37 persons and 90 others in Sarajevo in August 1995, NATO launched a large airstrike on Bosnian Serb Army positions. Between August 30 and September 14, four hundred NATO planes launched thousands of attacks against key Bosnian Serb military units and installations in Sarajevo, Pale, Lisina, and other sites.

Meanwhile, starting in the summer of 1995, Bosnian Croat and Bosniak armies had begun to take the initiative in the ground war against the Bosnian Serbs. The combined allied armies launched a series of offensives against Bosnian Serbs in western Bosnia. By the end of July, the allies had captured 1,600 square kilometers of territory. In the Krajina region, a massive Bosnian Croat-Bosniak offensive involving 170,000 soldiers, 250 tanks, 500 artillery pieces, and 40 planes overwhelmed the Bosnian Serb forces of 30,000 troops, 300 tanks, 200 armored carriers, 560 artillery pieces, 135 anti-aircraft guns, and 25 planes.

By October 12, Bosnian Serb-held Banja Luka was in sight. The Bosnian Croat-Bosniak offensives had captured western Bosnia and 51% of the country, and threatened to advance further east. By this time, Bosnian Serb forces were on the brink of defeat.

Representatives from the three ethnic groups now met to negotiate an end to the war. On September 14, NATO ended its air strikes against Bosnian Serb forces. By month's end, fighting was winding down in most sectors.

On November 21, 1995, high-level government officials from Bosnia-Herzegovina, Serbia, and Croatia signed a peace agreement, bringing the war to an end. The reconstruction of the war-ravaged country soon began.

Many atrocities and human rights violations were committed in the war, the great majority of which were perpetrated by Bosnian Serbs, but also by Bosnian Croats, and to a much lesser extent, by Bosniaks.

The International Criminal Tribunal for the Former Yugoslavia (ICTY), established by the UN to prosecute war crimes, determined that Bosnian Serb atrocities committed in the town of Srebrenica, where 8,000 civilians were killed, constituted a genocide. Other atrocities, such as the killing and wounding of over one hundred residents in Markale on February 5, 1994 and August 28, 1995 resulting from the Serbian mortar shelling of Sarajevo, have been declared by the ICTY as ethnic cleansing (a war crime less severe than genocide).

Map 12. Bosnian War. Some key battle sites are indicated. Serbia and Croatia, adjacent countries to Bosnia, were involved in the war since a sizable population of ethnic Croats and ethnic Serbs lived in Bosnia-Herzegovina.

Bosnian Croat forces also perpetrated many atrocities, including those that occurred in the Lasva Valley, which caused the deaths and forced disappearances of 2,000 Bosniaks, as well as other violent acts against civilians. Bosniak forces also committed crimes against civilians and captured soldiers, but these were of much less frequency and severity.

About 90% of all crimes in the Bosnian War were attributed to Bosnian Serbs. The ICTY has convicted and meted out punishments to many perpetrators, who generally were military commanders and high-ranking government officials. The war caused some 100,000 deaths, both civilian and military; over two million persons were displaced by the fighting.

After the war, Bosnia-Herzegovina retained its territorial integrity. As a direct consequence of the war, Bosnia-Herzegovina established a decentralized government composed of two political and geographical entities: the Republic of Bosnia and Herzegovina (consisting of Bosniak and Bosnian Croat majorities) and the Republic of Srpska (consisting of Bosnian Serbs). The president of Bosnian-Herzegovina is elected on rotation, with a Bosniak, Bosnian Croat, and Bosnian Serb taking turns as the country's head of state.

KOSOVO WAR

Background Kosovo is located at the southwestern section of Serbia. In 1945, while under Yugoslavia's communist rule, Kosovo was granted limited self-rule. In 1974, this limited self-rule was expanded when Kosovo was declared a province within Serbia, but with nearly the same political status as Yugoslavia's six constituent republics (Serbia, Slovenia, Croatia, Bosnia-Herzegovina, Montenegro, and Macedonia).

For much of the second half of the twentieth century, the fear of the Soviet Union, the unifying communist ideology, and Yugoslavia's charismatic leader, Josip Broz Tito, held Yugoslavia as a tight-knit political unit, practically erasing separatist sentiments among its many ethnic groups. With Tito's death in 1980, however, Yugoslavia began its descent into political anarchy, hastened greatly toward the end of the decade by regional developments, particularly the fragmenting Soviet Union, the end of the Cold War, and the demise of communism in Eastern Europe.

As in the other Yugoslav republics with mixed ethnic compositions, Kosovo saw the rise of nationalism along ethnic lines. Kosovo had two main ethnic groups: the majority Albanians (comprising 77% of the population) who desired greater autonomy from Serbia, and Kosovo Serbs (15% of the population) who wanted more political integration with Serbia.

The Kosovo government was controlled by Albanians, who generally also held greater local political power. In turn, Kosovo Serbs felt oppressed and persecuted by Kosovo Albanians. In early 1986, Kosovo Serbs began holding protest rallies and marches in Kosovo and Serbia, causing tensions to rise between them and Kosovo Albanians. By November 1988, these assemblies were being held in many cities and towns in Kosovo and were attended by hundreds of thousands of protesters.

Soon enough, the Kosovo government was overthrown. In its place, a pro-Serbia government was installed. In March 1989, the new government passed a constitutional amendment that reverted Kosovo to its pre-1974 status, that is, the end of Kosovo's expanded autonomy and the return to limited self-rule. In June 1989, the Serbian government approved this amendment in its new constitution.

With Kosovo's return to limited self-rule, the "Albanianization" program that had begun in the late 1960s was reversed: not only were Kosovo's political and independence aspirations suppressed by the new regime, but so were the Albanian culture, language, the media, and education. Already the poorest among Yugoslavia's political entities, Kosovo suffered more economic hardships under the new government, causing poverty and unemployment to soar and forcing tens of thousands to leave the country to find work abroad. The Albanians began conducting protest rallies and demonstrations, but these were answered with Serbian forces entering Kosovo and disarming the Albanian security units and taking over police duties.

Kosovo Albanian political leaders called for civil disobedience, urging Albanians to stop paying taxes and ignoring Serbia's mandatory military conscription. Despite Serbia's opposition, Kosovo Albanians held a referendum in September 1991, where the overwhelming majority voted for separation from Serbia. In May the following year, Kosovo Albanians formed a separate Kosovo government, which was rejected by Serbia.

War In April 1996, the Kosovo Liberation Army (KLA), an extremist Albanian militia that sought to gain Kosovo's independence by force, launched attacks against Serbian police units across Kosovo. By March 1988, as the KLA had grown in strength and were intensifying its armed operations, the Yugoslav Army entered Kosovo. Fighting occurred from March to September, concentrated mostly in central-south Kosovo. The Yugoslav Army was far superior in strength, forcing the KLA to resort to guerilla tactics, such as ambushing army and security patrols, and raiding isolated military outposts. Through a tactical war of attrition, the KLA gained control of Decani, Malisevo, Orahovac, Drenica Valley, and northwest Pristina (Map 13).

In September 1998, the Yugoslav Army and Kosovo Serb forces launched offensive operations in northern and central Kosovo, driving away the KLA from many areas. These offensives also turned 200,000 civilians into refugees, prompting the United Nations to call for a ceasefire and an end to the conflict.

With the North Atlantic Treaty Organization (NATO) threatening to intervene, Yugoslavia agreed to a ceasefire in October 1998. A multi-national observer team then arrived in Kosovo to monitor the ceasefire. Fighting broke out in December 1998, however, which escalated in intensity early the next year, forcing the multi-national observer team to leave Kosovo in March 1999.

NATO became increasingly involved in the war – especially after the discovery of the bodies of 45 executed Kosovo Albanian farmers – and decided that direct military intervention was needed to end the war. In March 1999, NATO presented to Yugoslavia a proposal to station 30,000 NATO soldiers in Kosovo to monitor and maintain peace. Furthermore, the NATO force was to have free, unrestricted passage across Yugoslavia. The Yugoslav government vehemently rejected the UN proposal, calling it a violation of Yugoslavia's territorial sovereignty. In turn, Yugoslavia offered its own peace proposal, which was also rejected by NATO. The diplomatic impasse prompted NATO to begin military action against Yugoslavia.

On March 23, 1999, using over one thousand planes, NATO began launching massive air strikes against military installations and facilities in Yugoslavia. Later, NATO targeted Yugoslav Army units as well. NATO planes also attacked public infrastructures such as roads, railways, bridges, telecommunications systems, power stations, schools, and hospitals. Many unintended targets were hit as well, such as a convoy of Kosovo Albanian refugees, a Kosovo prison, a Serbian television facility, and the Chinese Embassy in Belgrade. The NATO air attacks against non-military targets drew widespread international condemnation.

In retaliation for the air strikes, the Yugoslav Army and Kosovo Serb forces expelled Kosovo Albanians from their homes. Within a few weeks, some 750,000 Kosovo Albanians had been forced to flee to neighboring Albania, Macedonia, and Montenegro.

On June 3, the government of Yugoslavia, persuaded by Russia, yielded to strong international pressure and agreed to accept NATO's peace proposal. Thereafter, Yugoslav forces withdrew from Kosovo. NATO then ended its air strikes against Yugoslavia and sent a peacekeeping force, under a UN mandate, to enter Kosovo. Russia, which was Yugoslavia's staunchest supporter during the war, also deployed its own peacekeepers in Kosovo to serve as a foil against the NATO troops. NATO and Russian peacekeepers coordinated their actions, however, to secure peace in Kosovo while avoiding unwanted confrontations between them.

About 13,000 persons died in the Kosovo War. Over one million civilians fled the fighting and became refuges, although most eventually returned to their homes after the war. Perhaps as many as 200,000 ethnic Serbs fled Kosovo in the years after the war. Yugoslavian and

Kosovo Serbian political and military leaders, including KLA members, have been charged with war crimes.

In February 2008, Kosovo Albanians declared Kosovo an independent country. Serbia rejected Kosovo's independence and has since maintained its claim to Kosovo as being an integral part of Serbian territory. While the United States, United Kingdom, and other countries recognize Kosovo's independence, many others do not. Russia, in particular, insists that any proposed solution must be acceptable to both Serbia and Kosovo.

Map 13. Kosovo War. By using guerilla tactics, Kosovar insurgents gained control of portions of Kosovo.

NAGORNO-KARABAKH WAR

Background From early 1988 to May 1994, Azerbaijan's Nagorno-Karabakh region (Map 14) was the center of fighting between the ethnic Armenians who constituted the majority population in the region and the ethnic Azerbaijanis who comprised the second largest population. The Armenians wanted to merge Nagorno-Karabakh with the Republic of Armenia, while the Azerbaijanis desired that the region remain with the Republic of Azerbaijan. The Armenians were supported by the Republic of Armenia while the Azerbaijanis were backed by the Republic of Azerbaijan.

The origin of the war goes back to 1917, to events in Russia after the overthrow of the Tsarist government and the outbreak of the Russian Civil War. At that time, Armenia and Azerbaijan were ruled by Russia. Previously, Armenia had been under the domination of the Ottoman Empire, but fell to Russia in World War I. Azerbaijan was ruled by Persia until the 1800s when it came under the control of the Russian Empire.

Taking advantage of Russia's preoccupation with its civil war, Armenians and Azerbaijanis rose up in rebellion against Russian rule and subsequently formed two new countries, the Republic of Armenia and the Republic of Azerbaijan, respectively. Many regions in the two new countries contained large mixed populations of Armenians and Azerbaijanis. Although these endemic populations had lived together peacefully for centuries, ethnic tensions now rose between them. Ethnic tensions and an undefined border eventually led to war between Armenia and Azerbaijan.

After World War I, Britain briefly occupied Armenia and Azerbaijan (including Georgia to the north), with the aim of using the Caucasus region as a buffer zone against possible communist expansion should Russia fall to the Bolsheviks in the on-going Russian Civil War.

In 1921, the Bolsheviks did win the civil war. Consequently, the Soviets invaded and re-occupied the whole Caucasus region and established a satellite "Soviet Socialist Republic" in Georgia, Armenia, and Azerbaijan. The Soviets fixed the borders of the republics, and awarded Nagorno-Karabakh to Azerbaijan, despite the region containing a majority Armenian population. The Soviet policy was to polarize mixed populations in occupied territories in order to prevent any organized opposition to the national communist government.

During Soviet rule, the iron group of communism erased tensions between Armenians and Azerbaijanis, both of whom were united, together with the many other ethnic groups, under the monolithic hegemony of the USSR.

In 1985, the Soviet Union began to implement political and economic reforms. Consequently, a sea change swept across Eastern Europe, as Warsaw Pact countries shed communism and adopted democracy. By 1990, the Soviet Union was on the verge of collapse, and its many "satellite republics" were seceding and moving towards declaring independence.

The Soviet Union's decline roused nationalist sentiments in Armenian and Azerbaijan, as in all other Soviet states. In Yerevan, Armenia's capital, industrial workers staged strike actions against the communist government. Armenians took to the streets calling for Nagorno-Karabakh to be merged with Armenia. In response, Azerbaijanis demanded that Nagorno-Karabakh remain with

Azerbaijan. Ethnic tensions rose between Armenians and Azerbaijanis in Nagorno-Karabakh.

In February 1989, Mikhail Gorbachev, the Soviet Union's head of state, met with Armenian and Azerbaijani leaders and requested them to stop their protest actions pending a Soviet decision on the issue of Nagorno-Karabakh. The following month, the Soviet Union declared that Nagorno-Karabakh must remain with Azerbaijan.

Map 14. Armenia and Azerbaijan. The two countries fought a war over the Nagorno-Karabakh region.

Violence broke out in Nagorno-Karabakh, as well as in other parts of Armenia and Azerbaijan where mixed populations of the two ethnic groups also existed. For nearly the whole of 1988, civilian clashes broke out frequently, with both sides committing crimes and atrocities, such as murders, beatings, rapes, forced expulsions, lootings, and arson.

By January 1990, the persistent violence alarmed Soviet authorities, who ordered their security forces to intervene. With the arrival of Soviet forces in Nagorno-Karabakh, peace and order was restored – temporarily. Over the past several months, Nagorno-Karabakh Armenians and Azerbaijanis had begun preparations for war. Many were active or former Soviet Army servicemen who had acquired large stockpiles of weapons and ammunitions from many sources, including Soviet Army caches, donations from foreign donors, and direct purchases. During the period of the Soviet Union's disintegration, large amounts of Soviet weapons became readily available for sale directly from Soviet government officials and military officers, openly or from the black market.

War In early 1990, clashes broke out between units of the Armenian Army and Azerbaijani militias in several Azerbaijani enclaves inside Armenia. The Soviet Army intervened to prevent these enclaves from falling to the Armenians. By the end of 1991, the Soviet Union had ceased to exist. By then, Armenia and Azerbaijan had declared their independences one month apart of each other – they were now sovereign countries. With the end of the Soviet Union, Russian soldiers withdrew from Armenia and Azerbaijan, including Nagorno-Karabakh; the last Soviet soldiers departed from Nagorno-Karabakh in December 1991.

In November 1991, Azerbaijan officially declared that Nagorno-Karabakh was part of its territory. However, in a referendum held in Nagorno-Karabakh the following month, ethnic Armenians voted overwhelmingly to form a separate state. Nagorno-Karabakh Azerbaijanis boycotted the referendum. In June 1992, Nagorno-Karabakh broke away from Azerbaijan, with ethnic Armenians declaring independence as the Nagorno-Karabakh Republic.

Full-scale war broke out. Nagorno-Karabakh Armenians attacked and captured Khojali and Shusa in early 1991, and Lachin in May (Map

15); the latter's capture allowed Nagorno-Karabakh to be linked geographically to Armenia. Consequently, Armenian Army units began arriving in Nagorno-Karabakh. By the summer of 1992, Armenians had gained control of much of Nagorno-Karabakh. As Turkey was sympathetic to Azerbaijan, Armenia took the precaution against a Turkish invasion by joining the Conference of Independent States, a Russia-led alliance of former Soviet states.

Map 15. Nagorno-Karabakh. Some key battle sites during the Nagorno-Karabakh War.

By June 1992, the Azerbaijan Army had finalized plans for a counter-attack into Armenian-held Nagorno-Karabakh. Opening their offensive along four fronts, the Azerbaijanis were successful initially and captured many villages and a major town. They were stopped at Aghdara, however, after the Armenians merged many disparate militias into a single national army, called the Nagorno-Karabakh Republic Defense Army.

Following a lull during the winter, Armenian forces launched an offensive in early 1992. By May, the Armenians had recaptured most of the territories they had lost the previous year. Mediation efforts by many countries, including Iran, Russia, France, and the United States, failed to stop the fighting. The Azerbaijani offensives launched in June and August, 1992 failed to make significant headway. Later that year, the two sides settled down for the winter.

As in the previous winters of the war, food shortages made living conditions difficult in Nagorno-Karabakh and Armenia, as 85% of these regions' food supplies arrived from Azerbaijan by rail traffic, which had been closed down. The war also had a serious impact on Nagorno-Karabakh Azerbaijanis, thousands of whom had been displaced from their homes and had fled as refugees into makeshift camps inside Azerbaijan.

In early 1993, the Armenians resumed their offensive and recaptured portions of northern Nagorno-Karabakh that had fallen earlier to the Azerbaijanis. In April, Armenian forces captured Kalbajar, an Azerbaijani district outside Nagorno-Karabakh. The fall of Kalbajar sent shock waves all across Azerbaijan. A political crisis erupted, which led to a change in the government.

Kalbajar's capture was condemned by the United Nations Secretary General, who demanded that Armenia immediately withdraw its forces from the Azerbaijani district. The Armenians ignored the directive and pursued their offensive. By late summer of 1993, apart from controlling much of Nagorno-Karabakh, the Armenians had occupied 9% of Azerbaijan territory.

In July 1994, the Azerbaijan Army launched an offensive into Nagorno-Karabakh. The attack made some progress against the Nagorno-Karabakh Armenians but was stopped when the regular Armenian Army entered the fighting. The combined Armenian forces then launched a counter-attack. The Azerbaijanis failed to offer any effective opposition, as they were depleted of troops and ammunitions.

The Armenians had achieved success in the battlefield, but were facing serious internal problems, including a devastated economy, political infighting, and a population that was weary of the war. Exhausted by six years of fighting, representatives from all sides of the conflict met to negotiate a settlement. Under mediation efforts by Russia, the governments of Armenia, Azerbaijan, and Nagorno-Karabakh signed a peace agreement in May 1994.

FIRST CONGO WAR

During the First Congo War, the Central African country now known as the Democratic Republic of the Congo was known as Zaire (Map 16).

Background In the mid-1990s, ethnic tensions rose in Zaire's eastern regions. Zairian indigenous tribes long despised the Tutsis, another ethnic tribe, whom they regarded as foreigners, i.e. they believed that Tutsis were not native to the Congo. The Congolese Tutsis were called Banyamulenge and had migrated to the Congo during the pre-colonial and Belgian colonial periods. Over time, the Banyamulenge established some degree of political and economic standing in the Congo's eastern regions. Nevertheless, Zairian indigenous groups occasionally attacked Banyamulenge villages, as well as those of other non-Congolese Tutsis who had migrated more recently to the Congo.

During the second half of the twentieth century, the Congo's eastern region was greatly destabilized when large numbers of refugees migrated there to escape the ethnic violence in Rwanda and Burundi. The greatest influx occurred during the Rwandan Civil War, where some 1.5 million Hutu refugees entered the Congo's Kivu Provinces (Map 17). The Hutu refugees established giant settlement camps which soon came under the control of the deposed Hutu regime in Rwanda, the same government that had carried out the genocide against Rwandan Tutsis. Under cover of the camps, Hutu leaders organized a militia composed of former army soldiers and civilian paramilitaries. This Hutu militia carried out attacks against Rwandan Tutsis in the camps, as well as against the Banyamulenge, i.e.

Congolese Tutsis. The Hutu leaders wanted to regain power in Rwanda and therefore ordered their militia to conduct cross-border raids from the Zairian camps into Rwanda.

To counter the Hutu threat, the Rwandan government forged a military alliance with the Banyamulenge, and organized a militia composed of Congolese Tutsis. The Rwandan government-Banyamulenge alliance solidified in 1995 when the Zairian government passed a law that rescinded the Congolese citizenship of the Banyamulenge, and ordered all non-Congolese citizens to leave the country.

War In October 1996, the provincial government of South Kivu in Zaire ordered all Bayamulenge to leave the province. In response, the Banyamulenge rose up in rebellion. Zairian forces stepped in, only to be confronted by the Banyamulenge militia as well as Rwandan Army units that began an artillery bombardment of South Kivu from across the border.

A low-intensity rebellion against the Congolese government had already existed for three decades in Zaire. Led by Laurent-Désiré Kabila, the Congo rebels opposed Zairian president Mobutu Sese Seko's despotic, repressive regime. President Mobutu had seized power through a military coup in 1965 and had in his long reign, grossly mismanaged the country. Government corruption was widespread, the country's infrastructure was crumbling, and poverty and unemployment were rampant. And while Zaire's economy stagnated under a huge foreign debt, President Mobutu amassed a personal fortune of several billions of dollars.

Kabila joined his forces with the Banyamulenge militia; together, they united with other anti-Mobutu rebel groups in the Kivu, with the collective aim of overthrowing the Zairian dictator. Kabila soon became the leader of this rebel coalition. In December 1996, with the support of Rwanda and Uganda, Kabila's rebel forces won control of the border areas of the Kivu. There, Kabila formed a quasi-government that was allied to Rwanda and Uganda.

The Rwandan Army entered the conquered areas in the Kivu and dismantled the Hutu refugee camps in order to stop the Hutu militia from carrying out raids into Rwanda. With their camps destroyed, one batch of Hutu refugees, comprising several hundreds of thousands of civilians, was forced to head back to Rwanda.

Map 16. Africa showing location of the Democratic Republic of the Congo (DRC) and other African countries. At the time of the First Congo War, DRC was known as Zaire.

Another batch, also composed of several hundreds of thousands of Hutus, fled westward and deeper into Zaire, where many perished from diseases, starvation, and nature's elements, as well as from attacks by the Rwandan Army.

When the fighting ended, some areas of Zaire's eastern provinces virtually had seceded, as the Zairian government was incapable of mounting a strong military campaign into such a remote region. In fact, because of the decrepit condition of the Zairian Armed Forces, President Mobutu held only nominal control over the country.

Map 17. First Congo War. In the map D.R.C. refers to the Democratic Republic of the Congo.

The Zairian soldiers were poorly paid and regularly stole and sold military supplies. Poor discipline and demoralization afflicted the ranks, while corruption was rampant among top military officers.

Zaire's military equipment often was non-operational because of funding shortages. More critically, President Mobutu had become the enemy of Rwanda and Angola, as he provided support for the rebel groups fighting the governments in those countries. Other African countries that also opposed Mobutu were Eritrea, Ethiopia, Zambia, and Zimbabwe.

In December 1996, Angola entered the war on the side of the rebels after signing a secret agreement with Rwanda and Uganda. The Angolan government then sent thousands of ethnic Congolese soldiers called "Katangese Gendarmes" to the Kivu Provinces. These Congolese soldiers were the descendants of the original Katangese Gendarmes who had fled to Angola in the early 1960s after the failed secession of the Katanga Province from the Congo.

The presence of the Katangese Gendarmes greatly strengthened the rebellion: from Goma and Bukavu (Map 17), the Gendarmes advanced west and south to capture Katanga and central Zaire. On March 15, 1977, Kisangani fell to the rebels, opening the road to Kinshasa, Zaire's capital. Kalemie and Kamina in Katanga Province were captured, followed by Lubumbashi in April. Later that month, the Angolan Army invaded Zaire from the south, quickly taking Tshikapa, Kikwit, and Kenge.

Kabila also joined the fighting. Backed by units of the Rwandan and Ugandan Armed Forces, his rebel coalition force advanced steadily across central Zaire for Kinshasa. Kabila met only light resistance, as the Zairian Army collapsed, with desertions and defections widespread in its ranks. Crowds of people in the towns and villages welcomed Kabila and the foreign armies as liberators.

Many attempts were made by foreign mediators (United Nations, United States, and South Africa) to broker a peace settlement, the last occurring on May 16, 1977 when Kabila's forces had reached the vicinity of Kinshasa. The Zairian government collapsed, with President Mobutu fleeing the country. Kabila entered Kinshasa and formed a new government, and named himself president. The First Congo War was over; the second phase of the conflict broke out just 15 months later *(next article)*.

SECOND CONGO WAR

Background The First Congo War *(previous article)* ended when Laurent-Désiré Kabila took over power in Zaire. He formed a new government and named himself the country's president. He renamed the country the "Democratic Republic of the Congo". President Kabila faced enormous problems: the country's infrastructure was in ruins partly because of the war but mainly because of neglect by the previous regime; the economy was devastated; and most of the people lived in poverty.

And these were the least of President Kabila's problems. He was most concerned about his tenuous hold on power. He had merged his rebel forces with the Rwandan Army, which produced tensions between the two former enemies. Furthermore, some military officers remained loyal to ex-President Mobutu Sese Seko, the deposed tyrant.

To consolidate power, President Kabila set up an authoritarian regime, centralized power, and appointed relatives and friends to top government positions. His administration was accused of nepotism, abuse of power, and corruption, and President Kabila's critics drew similarities between his government and the former regime – implying that nothing had changed.

More crucial image-wise for President Kabila was the ubiquitous presence in the Congo of foreign troops, particularly those from Rwanda and Uganda; these countries had helped him win the First Congo War. The Congolese people perceived the foreign armies as holding real power in the country, with President Kabila merely acting as a figurehead. For this reason, on July 14, 1998, President Kabila sacked his Armed Forces chief of staff, a Rwandan, an act that began a chain of events that led to the Second Congo War.

On July 27, President Kabila ordered the Rwandan and Ugandan Armies to leave the country. A week later, he terminated the appointments of all Tutsi public officials. The Congolese people regarded the Tutsis as foreigners, despite the fact that Banyamulenge Tutsis were long established in the Congo's eastern provinces.

As a result of President Kabila's edict, Uganda pulled out its forces from the Congo. The Rwandan government also ordered its forces to withdraw, not out of the Congo, but to the remote, weakly defended Kivu Provinces in eastern Congo. Rwanda believed that its security concerns – the main reason for its involvement in the First Congo War – had not been fully met. In particular, the Rwandan government noted that the Hutu militias had reorganized and once again were carrying out raids into Rwanda. Furthermore, the Banyamulenge Tutsis, who had formed an alliance with Rwanda during the First Congo War, requested the Rwandans to remain in the Kivu Provinces. The Banyamulenge's citizenship had been revoked by a new law, and the Congolese government ordered them to leave the country.

Rwanda and Uganda organized the Banyamulenge into a proxy militia called the "Rally for Congolese Democracy", or RCD, whose aim was to overthrow President Kabila. As in the First Congo War, Rwanda and Uganda used a proxy force to fight their wars, as direct intervention by their armies was a violation of international law.

War On August 2, 1998, thousands of ethnic Tutsi soldiers in the Congolese Army mutinied in Kisangani, an event that triggered the Second Congo War. Within a few days, the mutiny had spread across the Congo's eastern region. The mutiny prompted Rwanda and

Uganda to mobilize the RCD, which was to act as a front for their armies to invade the Congo.

Fighting broke out in the Kivu Provinces, where Goma and Bukavu were easily overrun by the invading forces. Kisangani, prized for its rich mineral deposits, also was taken. (Map 18 shows the major battle sites during the Second Congo War.)

On August 4, a second invasion front was opened when Rwanda and Uganda airlifted two brigades of their soldiers to Kitona, located near the Congo's Atlantic coast. At Kitona, the invaders succeeded in winning over the local garrison consisting of 30,000 soldiers; they also seized battle tanks, heavy artillery, and other military hardware. The invaders also took control of the nearby towns of Moanda and Banana.

On August 10, the coalition forces comprising the foreign armies and the Congolese defectors moved out from Kitona, with Kinshasa, the Congo's capital, as their objective. Three days later, they captured Matadi, thereby cutting off the Congo's access to the Atlantic Ocean and threatening Kinshasa's food supply. Electricity to the capital was severed when the invaders captured the Inga Dam, Kinshasa's main power source.

President Kabila abandoned Kinshasa and moved his government to Katanga Province, located in the country's southeast region. With widespread defections undermining his army and his remaining loyal troops largely ineffective, President Kabila appealed for foreign support, mainly from the South African Development Community, or SADC, a regional security alliance of which the Congo was a member state. Angola and Zimbabwe – participants in the First Congo War – responded by assuring President Kabila of their military assistance, as did Namibia. Zambia pledged support by guaranteeing the safe passage of friendly foreign troops through its territory.

Zimbabwean deployment in Kinshasa was swift, with some elite units immediately clashing with the vanguard unit of the invasion forces at Kasangulu. At Kisantu, some 100 kilometers from Kinshasa, the Zimbabweans stopped an enemy offensive.

By August 24, the main invasion force had advanced to within 45 kilometers of Kinshasa, where it was spotted by air reconnaissance. The invasion force then fell into a trap, where Zimbabwean air and ground attacks destroyed the advancing tanks, trucks, and other armored vehicles. Still, remnants of the invasion force pressed on without their armor and finally reached Kinshasa Airport, despite being subjected to intense air attacks. Fighting broke out around Kinshasa during the last week of August, before the invaders were forced to pull out of the city. Then as more Zimbabwean Army units arrived in Kinshasa, the threat to the capital passed. With its defeat in the western front, the Ugandan-Rwandan alliance abandoned its plans to capture Kinshasa. Soon thereafter, President Kabila returned his government to the capital.

By this time, Angolan forces also had come to the aid of President Kabila's beleaguered regime, entering through the Angolan province of Cabinda. The Angolans took control of the Congo's western region, including liberating the towns of Matadi and Kitona, and moved eastward to meet up with the Zimbabwean Army in Kinshasa. More Zimbabwean forces began pouring in via Zambia into southern Congo, with the aim of securing Mbuji-Mayi, a diamond-rich mining town in Kasai-Oriental Province. With military forces from Namibia deploying in the western Congo and those from Chad entering through the north, both in support of the Congolese government, and Burundi, backing the invaders, the conflict threatened to widen into a full-blown multinational war (in fact, the war has been called "Africa's World War").

With Kinshasa secure by early September, the Angola-Zimbabwe-Congo coalition made plans to launch an offensive into rebel-held territories further east. Rwanda and Uganda had recruited extensively – some 100,000 new soldiers were brought to the frontlines, greatly overmatching in numbers the combined Angolan-Zimbabwean forces (the latter, however, consisted mainly of elite combat units). Both sides of the conflict also increased the strength of their battle tanks, armored vehicles, artillery, and warplanes.

In the following months, a number of indecisive battles took place, as each side tried to expand its control in northern Katanga Province and in central Congo. In northern Congo, the Ugandan Army organized the Movement for the Liberation of the Congo, a proxy militia, to serve as its advance force in its offensive into northeast Congo.

In March 1999, the Rwandan Army, spearheaded by its RCD proxy militia, launched a three-pronged attack into northern Katanga, meeting the Zimbabwean Army in battles around Kgala, Kongolo, and Pweto. A few weeks later, another Rwandan operation advanced deep into Kasai-Oriental, but just came short of its objective, Mbuji-Mayi.

By mid-1999, the battle lines of the war had settled, essentially carving the country into three broad zones of control: those that were government-controlled, Uganda-aligned, and Rwanda-aligned. In areas where it had lost control, the Congolese government organized armed resistance groups consisting of indigenous tribes and anti-Rwanda Hutus to defend Congolese villages and repel Rwandan and Ugandan proxy militias.

In April 1999, the governments of the Congo and Uganda signed a ceasefire agreement, which had the unexpected consequence of abruptly ending the Uganda-Rwanda alliance. Relations became strained between the erstwhile allies, which worsened to the point that the Ugandan-Rwandan joint governance of the main proxy force, the RCD, fell apart. Consequently, the RCD split into two factions, one aligned with each of the two former allies.

Map 18. Second Congo War.

Then in July 1999, under the auspices of the United Nations, Organization of African Unity, and the SADC, the warring countries met in Lusaka, Zambia and agreed to a ceasefire (called the Lusaka Ceasefire Agreement). The following month, a UN delegation of 90 personnel arrived in the Congo to monitor the ceasefire; the UN mission was enlarged to over 5,000 members in February 2000. Initially, the ceasefire agreement was not fully implemented, as a flurry of accusations and counter-accusations of violations were raised by all sides. Some fighting also broke out, but on a much smaller scale.

Then, the war took a surprising turn when the Rwandan and Ugandan Armies, including their proxy militias, turned against each other and fought a series of bitter clashes in and around Kisangani. The point of contention in this "war within a war" was for control over the mineral resources in Orientale Province. The fighting in August 1999 was repeated in May and June the following year, with the Rwandans ultimately prevailing and taking control of Kisangani. Diplomatically, the clashes were a disaster for Rwanda and Uganda, as both countries' involvement in the war was supposedly to secure their borders, and yet they were fighting each other deep in the Congo.

Ironically, the Congolese government itself seemed averse to the Lusaka Ceasefire Agreement, as President Kabila was determined to use force to expel the invaders and reclaim all Congo territory. With the arrival of newly purchased weapons in 2000, the Congolese Army launched two major offensive operations. Both failed miserably, not least because of the continued demoralized, ill-trained, and poorly paid conditions of the Congolese soldiers.

In January 2001, President Kabila was assassinated. His son, Joseph, took over the reins of government as the country's new president. The younger Kabila proved much more conciliatory to the Congo's enemies than his father was, and was determined to end the war. The new president immediately opened peace negotiations with all warring sides. Later that year, his efforts bore fruit when the Congolese government signed peace agreements with Rwanda and Uganda, in July and September, respectively. In the agreements, Rwanda and Uganda promised to withdraw their forces from the Congo, while the Congolese government pledged to guarantee the security of its shared border with Rwanda and Uganda. The agreement also stipulated that the Congo would establish diplomatic relations with Rwanda and Uganda. With Rwanda particularly, President Kabila vowed to break up the anti-Rwanda Hutu militias in the Congo and thwart their attempts to launch raids into Rwanda.

The three sides carried out their parts of the agreements, bringing the war to an end. One major reason that the peace held was that President Kabila, under a stipulation of the Lusaka Ceasefire Agreement, was required to shed off his government's autocratic rule in order to bring about security and stability in the region. Furthermore, the fighting had ended in a stalemate, and the belligerents were unwilling to commit more resources to a protracted war. Just as important, the RCD – the proxy militia that had done much of the fighting for Rwanda and Uganda – was wracked with internal division and yearned for an end to the war. Furthermore, some sections of the Congo, especially the western and southern regions, had begun to stabilize. The arrival of foreign aid and international investments to the Congo were helping to improve the local economy and boost the government's credibility.

In April 2001, the Congo began its transition to democracy. A new constitution was passed, political parties were allowed to organize, and elections were scheduled. A transitional government in the Congo was formed on July 18, 2003 – the date generally designated as the end of the war. Some regional disturbance persisted, which forced the government to move the elections a year later, from 2005 to 2006. Democratic elections were held in July 2006, the first since 1960, with Kabila winning the presidential race.

The peace agreements that were intended to end the war did terminate large-scale fighting. Nevertheless, a low-intensity conflict persists in the Congo's eastern region, a major hotspot in the Second Congo War and where the government's authority is still undermined, giving the impression that the war has not truly ended. In the Kivu Provinces, despite the end of the Congo's support, Hutu militias continue to launch attacks into Rwanda. Furthermore, in the Ituri region in the Congo's northeast (Map 18), a combination of ethnic conflicts, land disputes, the presence of armed groups, and the repercussions of the two Congo Wars have turned this territory into a hotbed of unrest. At the heart of these conflicts, as often is the case with the Congo's past troubles, is the struggle for control over the country's vast mineral resources.

ANGOLAN WAR OF INDEPENDENCE

Background In the late 1400s, Portuguese merchant ships established trading relations with the Kingdom of Congo in West Africa. Then in 1575, the Portuguese built a settlement in the area of what is present-day Luanda (the Portuguese named the settlement *São Paulo da Assumpção de Loanda*), starting their involvement in the region that became their future colony of Angola. During the next 300 years, the Portuguese founded more settlements, as well as fortifications, along the African Atlantic coast.

The Portuguese continued trading relations with the Kingdom of Congo, and built new trading ties with the other tribal kingdoms in the area. They traded European firearms for the natives' ivory, minerals, and – of paramount importance in later periods – slaves. Slave trading in Luanda and other Portuguese ports became important for Portugal in its development of its prized colony of Brazil, and for its huge profits in filling the big demand for manpower in other New World jurisdictions.

Portuguese settlements were situated along the coast, with few settlers venturing into the African interior. Then in the 1880s, other European powers were jockeying aggressively to gain a share of the large continent, this so-called "Scramble for Africa" soon leading to Africa being carved up into European colonies. As a result of many treaties signed among the competing European powers, the borders of the African colonies were fixed, with colonial rights for Angola being assigned to Portugal.

By the 1830s, Portugal had lost Brazil and had abolished its transatlantic slave trade. To replace these two valuable sources of income, Portugal turned to develop its African possessions, including their interior lands. In Angola, agriculture was developed, with the valuable export crops of coffee and cotton being grown in vast plantations. The mining industry was expanded.

Portugal's development of the local economy, including the construction of public infrastructures such as roads and bridges, was carried out using forced labor of black Africans, a system that was so harsh, ruthless, and akin to slavery. Consequently, thousands of natives fled from the colony. Indigenous lands were seized by the colonial government. And while Angola's economy grew, only the colonizers benefited, while the overwhelming majority of natives were neglected and deprived of education, health care, and other services.

After World War II, thousands of Portuguese immigrants settled in Angola. The world's prices of coffee beans were high, prompting the Portuguese government to seek new white settlers in its African colonies to lead the growth of agriculture. However, many of the new arrivals settled in the towns and cities, instead of braving the harsh rural frontiers. In urban areas, they competed for jobs with black Angolans who likewise were migrating there in large numbers in search of work. The Portuguese, being white, were given employment preference over the natives, producing racial tension.

The late 1940s saw the rapid growth of nationalism in Africa. In Angola, three nationalist movements developed, which were led by "assimilados", i.e. the few natives who had acquired the Portuguese language, culture, education, and religion. The Portuguese officially designated "assimilados" as "civilized", in contrast to the vast majority of natives who retained their indigenous lifestyles.

The first of these Angolan nationalist movements was the People's Movement for the Liberation of Angola or MPLA (Portuguese: *Movimento Popular de Libertação de Angola*) led by local communists, and formed in 1956 from the merger of the Angolan Communist Party and another nationalist movement called PLUA (English: Party of the United Struggle for Africans in Angola). Active in Luanda and other major urban areas, the MPLA drew its support from the local elite and in regions populated by the Ambundu ethnic group. In its formative years, it received foreign support from other left-wing African nationalist groups that were also seeking the independences of their colonies from European rule. Eventually, the MPLA fell under the influence of the Soviet Union and other communist countries.

The second Angolan nationalist movement was the National Front for the Liberation of Angola or FNLA (Portuguese: *Frente Nacional de Libertação de Angola*). The FNLA was formed in 1962 from the merger of two Bakongo regional movements that had as their secondary aim the resurgence of the once powerful but currently moribund Kingdom of Congo. Primarily, the FNLA wanted to end forced labor, which had caused hundreds of thousands of Bakongo natives to leave their homes. The FNLA operated out of Leopoldville (present-day Kinshasa) in the Congo from where it received military and financial support from the Congolese government. The FNLA was led by Holden Roberto, whose authoritarian rule and one-track policies caused the movement to experience changing fortunes during the coming war, and also bring about the formation of the third of Angola's nationalist movements, UNITA.

UNITA or National Union for the Total Independence of Angola (Portuguese: *União Nacional para a Independência Total de Angola*) was founded by Jonas Savimbi, a former high-ranking official of the FNLA, over disagreements with Roberto. Unlike the FNLA and MPLA, which were based in northern Angola, UNITA operated in the colony's central and southern regions and gained its main support from the Ovibundu people and other smaller ethnic groups. Initially,

UNITA embraced Maoist socialism but later moved toward West-allied democratic Africanism.

War of Independence On February 3, 1961, farm laborers in Baixa do Cassanje, Malanje, rose up in protest over poor working conditions. The protest quickly spread to many other regions, engulfing a wide area. The Portuguese were forced to send warplanes that strafed and firebombed many native villages. Soon, the protest was quelled.

Map 19.Africa showing location of present-day Angola and other African countries that were involved in the Angolan War of Independence. South-West Africa (present-day Namibia) was then under South African rule.

Occurring almost simultaneously with the workers' protest, armed bands (believed to be affiliated with the MPLA) carried out attacks in Luanda, particularly in the prisons and police stations, aimed at freeing political prisoners. The raids were repelled, with dozens of attackers and some police officers killed. In reprisal, government forces and Portuguese vigilante groups attacked Luanda's slums, where they killed thousands of black civilian residents.

In March 1961, Roberto led thousands of fighters of the UPA (Union of Peoples of Angola, a precursor organization of the FNLA) into northern Angola, where he incited the farmers to rise up in revolt. Violence soon broke out, where native farmers killed hundreds of Portuguese civilians, burned farms, looted property, and destroyed government infrastructures.

By May, the Portuguese government in Lisbon had sent thousands of soldiers to Angola. In a brutal counter-insurgency campaign, Portuguese troops killed more than 20,000 black civilians and razed the northern countryside. By year's end, the colonial government had quelled the uprising and pushed Holden and his UPA followers across the border to the Congo. Some 200,000 black Angolans also fled to the Congo to escape the fighting and government retribution.

Portugal's counter-insurgency methods were condemned by the international community. As a consequence of the uprisings, Portugal began to implement major reforms in Angola, as well as in its other African colonies. Forced labor was abolished, as was the arbitrary seizure of indigenous lands. Also for the first time, public education, health care, and other social services were expanded to the general population.

From the rebels' viewpoint, however, the Portuguese acts of reconciliation were too little and too late. The insurgency persisted, although with little success. The rebels' inability to expand the conflict resulted from a number of factors: the Portuguese Army's effective counter-insurgency campaign, the colonial government's successful socio-economic programs for the indigenous population, and the Angolan nationalist movements' failure to form a unified front.

By 1962, the FNLA had become the most dominant of the three nationalist movements. Roberto formed a government-in-exile (called *Govêrno revolucionário de Angola no exílio*) in Leopoldville, an astute political move as his nationalist aspirations gained recognition and financial support from the Organization of African Unity, or OAU. He continued to reject the offers from the MPLA to form a united front against the Portuguese.

In 1962, the MPLA came under the command of Agostinho Neto, who began to strengthen the movement's military capability despite the somewhat lackluster support provided by the Soviet Union, its main backer. The MPLA faced many challenges that threatened its survival. For instance, Leopoldville, where its headquarters was located, became increasingly inhospitable when the government in Congo-Leopoldville threw its support behind the FNLA. Consequently, the MPLA was forced to move to nearby Congo-Brazzaville, where the Marxist government there allowed Neto to establish his new headquarters. Furthermore, the MPLA was wracked by an internal power struggle, causing the movement to split into three competing factions. Because it embraced staunchly communist teachings, the MPLA was the ideological enemy of the other nationalist movements, particularly the FNLA (UNITA advocated Maoist socialism only moderately). The FNLA, wanting to eliminate its rivals, sent its militia against the MPLA, which led to armed clashes and generated bitter hostility between the two nationalist movements. Armed confrontations also occurred between the MPLA and UNITA when an MPLA faction entered Angola's eastern region, which was traditionally controlled by Savimbi.

Compared to the FNLA and MPLA, UNITA possessed only a small armed wing and consequently was the least militant of the three nationalist movements. Through this policy, UNITA hoped to win greater popular support and international sympathy. Nevertheless, UNITA did conduct a number of attacks, the most notorious being sabotaging the operations of the economically important Benguela Railway, which led to armed clashes with Portuguese forces in December 1996, where some 300 UNITA fighters were killed. UNITA's disruption of the Benguela Railway also angered the governments of Congo-Kinshasa and Zambia, which used this rail line to transport their mined copper.

By the early 1970s, the Portuguese had largely suppressed the insurrection, had expelled the rebels from Angola, and were making great strides to improve the local economy. In Portugal, however, the security situation was different, as the mother country was ready to implode. Not only were the Portuguese fighting in Angola, they were also trying to quell similar nationalist rebellions in Mozambique and Portuguese Guinea. The unpopular wars had already claimed the lives of 8,000 Portuguese soldiers as well as wounding 15,000 others, and were taking up 50% of the national budget to support 148,000 Portuguese soldiers fighting abroad.

On April 25, 1974, Portuguese Prime Minister Marcelo Caetano was ousted in a military coup. A military junta formed a new government which, by July 1974, had begun the process of ending the colonial wars and granting independence to Portugal's African colonies. Then in the succeeding months, Portuguese colonial forces and the African nationalist militias desisted from further engagements in battle.

In Angola, Portugal signed separate peace treaties with UNITA in June 1974, and the FNLA and MPLA in October 1974. Zaire and Zambia brought together the three Angolan nationalist movements in an attempt to forge unity. The agreements arising from these meetings did not last, however, as fighting among the rival nationalist movements continued.

Portugal wanted to turn over political power to a united Angola. In January 1975, the Portuguese government met with the leaders of the three Angolan nationalist movements in a series of negotiations in Alvor, Portugal. These negotiations resulted in the signing of the Alvor Agreement, which contained several provisions. First, Angola's independence was set for November 11, 1975. Second, during the ten-month interim period before independence, the three nationalist movements would form a power-sharing government to lead the country, with the local Portuguese High Commissioner acting as the mediator for disputes. Third, a national constitution would be drafted, and parliamentary elections would be held in October 1975. Fourth, the nationalist groups' armed wings would be integrated into the Portuguese colonial army; after the Portuguese had withdrawn from Angola, the core of Angola's Armed Forces would have been formed.

Consequently, the Angolan nationalists formed a coalition government which, however, proved ineffective and barely functioned. Furthermore, none of the other provisions of the Alvor Agreement was truly implemented. And just as the Alvor Agreement ended Portugal's war in Angola, it also sparked the so-called "decolonization war" (the hostilities during the interim period before Angola's independence) among the three Angolan nationalist movements, particularly between FNLA and MPLA. Shortly after Portugal had set the date for Angola's independence, the Angolan nationalist movements began aggressive recruitment campaigns and sought more weapons deliveries from their foreign backers.

Earlier in June 1971, the MPLA had gained considerable political leverage after it was recognized officially by the OAU, which also withdrew its support for the FNLA. During this time, the MPLA fell completely under the Soviet sphere of influence, while the FNLA drew closer to the United States and other Western countries. And as Portugal disengaged from Africa, Angola was transformed into a battleground of the Cold War, with the Angolan nationalist movements relegated to acting as proxy forces for the world's superpowers. China backed the West-aligned FNLA, an apparent contradiction, but this came about because the Soviet Union supported the MPLA, and relations between the two giant communist states were strained. Furthermore, U.S.-China diplomatic relations were improving.

Decolonization War In February 1975, armed clashes broke out in Luanda between two MPLA forces, with the main faction defeating a splinter group. The FNLA, which had built up its presence in Luanda, joined the fray against the MPLA. Fighting spread throughout most of the country, but centered mainly in the central and northern regions, with the FNLA initially getting the better of the MPLA. The Portuguese government in Angola condemned the outbreak of fighting but was unwilling to intervene, as it was preparing to leave the colony.

By July 1975, the tide of war had turned in favor of the MPLA. Neto's forces had defeated the FNLA in a number of battles in Luanda, thereby gaining control of the capital. The MPLA pushed the FNLA toward the Zairian border and was eroding at UNITA strongholds in the central regions. The MPLA had benefited from Portuguese High Commissioner Antonio Rosa Coutinho, a socialist, who provided Neto's forces with Portuguese weapons stockpiles in Angola.

With the MPLA victory looming before Angola's independence, the U.S. Central Intelligence Agency (CIA) became alarmed at a possible Marxist victory in East Africa. The CIA increased arms deliveries to the FNLA, and began to support UNITA, which had by this time, cast away its socialist leanings in favor of a decidedly African-centered democratic ideology.

Because of the fighting, the Portuguese government repealed the Alvor Agreement, which in any case, already had ceased to exist. Although still legally holding colonial power, Portugal was incapable and unwilling to intervene in the conflict.

As Portugal's involvement diminished, the Republic of South Africa, Angola's southern neighbor, became involved in the decolonization war – South African involvement in Angola would be significant for the next twelve years.

South Africa was then a white-minority rule apartheid state; it began its involvement in Angola as a military alliance with the fellow-white Portuguese colonial government to help each other stamp out nationalist rebellions in their respective territories. While Portugal was fighting the three Angolan nationalist movements (FNLA, MPLA, and UNITA), South Africa was involved in a war against SWAPO, or the South West African People's Organization, a nationalist movement that was seeking the independence of South-West Africa (present-day Namibia), which had been annexed by the South Africans in 1915.

The MPLA's territorial gains in central Angola prompted South Africa to intercede on behalf of UNITA. The South Africans were concerned that a victory by the Marxist MPLA in Angola would allow a communist toehold in West Africa. The South Africans, therefore, forged an alliance with the West-aligned UNITA (and FNLA) to allow a democratic government to form in Angola.

After receiving new American weapons, the FNLA began its offensive in August 1975 from its bases in northern Angola. Soon reinforced by Zairian Army units, the combined force defeated the MPLA in a number of battles and came to within thirty kilometers of its ultimate objective, Luanda.

Map 20. Angolan War of Independence. Major areas of military operations by Angolan nationalist militias as well as by expeditionary forces from Zaire, South Africa, and Cuba.

In August 1975, a South African Army unit crossed into southern Angola and secured the Cunene River Hydroelectric Dam complex. South Africa had constructed the facility to supply electricity to northern South-West Africa.

Then in October 1975, a South African invasion force invaded Cuando Cubango Province in Angola's southeast region. The FNLA and UNITA joined the South African offensive. Three other South African Army battle groups invaded as well, and the combined forces quickly captured a large swathe of Angolan territory within a few weeks, including the strategic cities and towns of Nova Lisboa (present-day Huambo), Roçadas (Xangongo), Sá da Bandeira (Lubango), and Moçâmedes (Namibe).

The South African-led offensive from the south and the FNLA advances from the north placed MPLA-held Luanda in grave danger. At this point, Marxist Cuba entered the war on the MPLA side to serve as a counterbalance against South Africa's support for UNITA and FNLA. Cuba's involvement in Angola began in July 1975 when a few Cuban military advisers arrived in Luanda to train MPLA fighters in the use of advanced Soviet weapons. Then in October 1975 as the decolonization war was expanding considerably, hundreds of Cuban Army elite personnel established training schools in and around Luanda to form and organize the MPLA Armed Forces.

The South Africans tried to conceal their involvement and originally were misidentified as white mercenaries fighting for UNITA and FNLA. Positive identification of the South Africans was made after an armed clash in Catengue on November 3, causing Neto to appeal to Cuba and the Soviet Union for greater military assistance. Cuba's response was swift: just four days later, on November 7, large numbers of Cuban troops began arriving in Luanda. Cuba's military deployment in Angola soon grew in size to be more than a match against the South African force. The Soviets also increased their arms shipments, which were already substantial. The Russian weapons included hundreds of battle tanks, armored vehicles, and artillery pieces, as well as several warplanes.

To meet the expected FNLA advance from the east, the MPLA hastily fortified Quifangondo, an interposing town some 30 kilometers north of Luanda. Roberto was intent on capturing Luanda before November 11, Angola's independence day. On November 10, he and 2,000 FNLA fighters, which included Zairian Army units and a South African artillery team, began advancing toward the capital. Before reaching Quifangondo, however, they fell into a trap, where the MPLA-Cuban artillery batteries opened fire with multiple rocket launchers, rocket grenades, howitzers, and mortars. Within an hour, in what is now called the "Battle of Death Road", the FNLA forces were destroyed, with hundreds of casualties lying dead on the battlefield and survivors retreating in confusion. The South African artillery unit, using antiquated guns that had been effective in earlier battles, was outgunned by the MPLA-Cuban batteries. Unknown at that time, in the face of this crushing defeat, Roberto and his once-dominant FNLA ceased to be of any major importance for the rest of the war.

On November 10, one day before Angola's independence, the Portuguese High Commissioner and members of the remaining Portuguese colonial government departed from the colony. In the months leading up to independence, hundreds of thousands of Portuguese civilians left Angola to escape the violence. These Portuguese nationals comprised nearly the whole colonial bureaucracy, the business and landowner classes, and skilled and unskilled workers. About one million Portuguese expatriates returned to their mother country following the independences of Angola, Mozambique, and Guinea-Bissau (Portuguese Guinea).

On November 11, 1975 in ceremonies at Luanda, the MPLA declared the independence of Angola and the formation of a socialist state. A government was formed with Neto becoming Angola's first president. The FNLA and UNITA also held separate independence ceremonies, at Huambo and Ambriz, respectively. Shortly thereafter, the FNLA and UNITA formed a coalition government with a power-sharing structure. The FNLA-UNITA government failed to draw widespread recognition, however, as President Neto consolidated power in Luanda.

After defeating Roberto's FNLA forces in the north, the Cuban-MPLA Army now directed its attention to the more dangerous South African-led coalition invasion in the south, which had come to within 300 kilometers of Luanda. At the approaches to Novo Redondo (Sumbe) and other strategic locations, the MPLA destroyed bridges.

Other MPLA units strengthened defensive positions. On November 25, Cuban artillery batteries stopped a South African-led attack on Ebo. The South Africans had planned to take Luanda before Angola's independence day. After failing in this objective, by December 1975, the South Africans and their Angolan allies had refocused their efforts to capturing as much territory as possible.

In January 1976, a Cuban-MPLA offensive to the south forced the South Africans to gradually cede territory. Other developments also were weighing against South Africa's involvement in Angola. For instance, the United Nations Security Council and the OAU, after discovering South Africa's involvement, condemned the invasion and put diplomatic pressure on South Africa to withdraw from Angola. Furthermore, after CIA involvement was exposed, the United States withdrew its support for the FNLA and UNITA, jeopardizing the American-South African tacit tactical alliance. The Americans' abrupt turn-around diplomatically isolated the South Africans even more.

By late March 1975, South Africa had withdrawn all its forces from Angola. Cuba also reduced its troop deployment, but kept a sizable military presence to safeguard Angola's security and maintain a stabilizing counterbalance against enemy forces in the region. With the FNLA forced out of the country and UNITA reduced to operating in the remote countryside, the MPLA government gained control over most of the country. In 1976, Angola was admitted to the United Nations and OAU, further legitimizing the MPLA's authority.

The Angolan nationalists triumphed in their war of independence against the Portuguese colonizers. On the larger, global stage, however, the Cold War was raging. The Angolan war did not end but segued into a civil war *(next article)*, dictated as much by the local partisan conflict as by the world's superpowers using their Angolan proxy armies to fight it out on this African battlefield.

ANGOLAN CIVIL WAR

After emerging victorious in the Angolan War of Independence, the People's Movement for the Liberation of Angola (MPLA) declared the independence of Angola and formed a Marxist government under President Agostinho Neto *(previous article)*. During the war, the arrival of many Cuban troops and large Soviet arms shipments turned the MPLA's near certain defeat into a complete victory. Consequently, the new Angolan government fell under the sphere of influence of its communist benefactors.

The two other Angolan nationalist movements, the National Front for the Liberation of Angola (FNLA) and the National Union for the Total Independence of Angola (UNITA), were defeated and nearly annihilated. The FNLA was pushed out of Angola and thereafter ceased to be a viable fighting force, while UNITA was forced into the far reaches of the country's southeastern region. In the context of the Cold War, the FNLA and UNITA were aligned with the democratic West and obtained their main support from the Republic of South Africa, and to some extent from the United States. However, the sudden end of U.S. support and the withdrawal of South African forces from Angola (after the discovery of their involvement in the Angolan War of Independence) led to the defeat of the FNLA and UNITA.

The Angolan War of Independence ended in March 1976. The new Angolan government quickly consolidated power, and by early 1977, had gained control over most of the country. In May 1977, a military-backed coup attempt was made against President Neto. Cuban forces intervened, saving the incumbent regime. In the aftermath, President Neto carried out a bloody purge of disloyal party members. Some 20,000 to 70,000 MPLA dissidents were killed during the next several months.

Despite its defeat, the FNLA continued a low-intensity insurgency war against Angola's government, with the support of its long-time backer, Zaire. Consequently, relations between Angola and Zaire were strained. In turn, Angola provided support for the Front for the National Liberation of the Congo (FNLC), an insurgency movement fighting to overthrow the Zairian government. In March 1977 and again in May 1978, FNLC fighters from eastern Angola invaded parts of Katanga Province in southeastern Zaire. In both instances, the arrival of foreign troops, especially the French, helped the Zairian Army to repel the invaders.

After the MPLA won the Angolan War of Independence, Cuba retained a sizable military presence in Angola to serve as a deterrent against an invasion by outside forces, especially by the South African Army. The Cuban presence was also in keeping with Fidel Castro's policy of assisting African nationalist movements in their "revolutionary struggles". The Cubans and the Angolan government built several military bases in Angola to train the South West African People's Organization (SWAPO), a nationalist movement fighting for the independence of South-West Africa (present-day Namibia) and MK (Zulu: *Umkhonto we Sizwe*, translated as "Spear of the Nation"), the armed wing of the African National Congress, an anti-apartheid nationalist movement in South Africa.

To counter the SWAPO and MK threats, South Africa strengthened its alliance with and support for UNITA. The idea was that South Africa would help UNITA overthrow the Angolan government, while UNITA would assist the South Africans defeat SWAPO and MK. American President Jimmy Carter's administration had been barred by U.S. Congress from further providing funding to

UNITA and FNLA. The U.S. government's support continued to reach the Angolan rebels, however, through American allies, such as Israel.

In 1977 and 1978, SWAPO insurgents from bases in southern Angola launched guerilla raids into northern South-West Africa. In response, the South Africans attacked and destroyed these SWAPO bases. (Map 21 shows the major battle areas during the Angolan Civil War.) In May 1978, the South Africans conducted large-scale operations in central southern Angola, including ground sweeps in Chetequera and a paratrooper raid in Cassinga. As a result, many SWAPO bases were destroyed. However, many civilians also were killed during these attacks, generating international condemnation and a number of United Nations Security Council resolutions against South Africa. Consequently, the South Africans were forced to scale back their operations. Meanwhile, the South African offensives had allowed UNITA to gain control of large sections of Angola's Cuando Cubango Province in 1979.

The UN had tried in vain to force an end to the war in order to allow the warring sides to negotiate a peaceful settlement. One reason for the UN failure was that South Africa opposed the independence of South-West Africa (as proposed by the UN), which the South African government had designated as a buffer zone against the anticipated spread of communism from Angola.

In June 1980, four South African battle groups advanced 260 kilometers into Angola's Chifufua complex to destroy SWAPO's command and logistical bases. The South Africans encountered some strong opposition, including meeting a mechanized enemy force, but succeeded in destroying SWAPO bases and seizing weapons stockpiles. Then in August 1981, the South Africans raided Xangongo and Ongiva, where they destroyed more SWAPO camps and captured heavy military hardware that included battle tanks, armored vehicles, trucks, and artillery pieces.

These successes brought large sections of Angola's Cunene Province under South African and UNITA control. Aided by UNITA, South African forces carried out mopping up operations further north where SWAPO units had retreated. UNITA also extended its operations north of Cuando Cubango Province and disrupted the operations of the commercially vital Benguela Railway.

In December 1983, a South African military operation into Cuvelai was resisted by the Angolan Army which, by this time, had built its bases near SWAPO camps. Even with the use of air support, the South African ground offensives at Cahama, Mulondo, and Caundo failed to break the Angolan Army-SWAPO defenses. Finally, the attack was called off.

In early 1984, the Angolan government reinforced the defenses of the southern territories still under its control. However, in May to September, 1984, representatives of Angola and South Africa held a number of dialogues to try and work out a peaceful settlement to the conflict. The meetings failed to achieve anything substantial, one reason being that Cuba, a major player in the conflict, was not involved in the negotiations.

In the mid-1980s, heightened tensions indicated an escalation of the war, because of the following reasons. First, U. S. president Ronald Reagan, a staunch anti-communist, renewed military funding for UNITA after the U.S. Congress approved government support for pro-democracy movements in Angola. Second, the Soviet Union increased its arms shipments to Angola. Third, the Angolan government was alarmed at UNITA's successes in southern Angola and wanted to square off with the rebels in a decisive battle.

Map 21. Angolan Civil War. The exclave Angolan province of Cabinda is shown at the top left.

In 1985, Soviet and East German military officers drew up plans for a large-scale military offensive into UNITA-occupied areas in southern Angola. The operation was intended to crush UNITA and drive out the South Africans from Angola. Then in August 1985, under the command of a Soviet general, Angolan-Cuban military units advanced toward Cuando Cubango Province, UNITA's stronghold. The offensive consisted of two columns advancing toward separate targets: one heading northwest for Cazombo to serve as a feint, and another pushing for Mavinga, which was the real objective. The capture of Mavinga and its prized airbases would allow Cuban planes to project into Jamba, UNITA's capital, and also challenge the South Africans' air domination in southern Angola. The Angolan-Cuban northern spearhead captured Cazombo, but its southern advance to Mavinga was repulsed by the South Africans' fierce air strikes and artillery bombardment. Consequently, the Angolan-Cuban forces were forced to turn back in defeat.

In May 1986, another Cuban-Angolan mechanized offensive to Cuando Cubango Province gained momentum initially, but strong South African-UNITA resistance forced the attackers to withdraw to the town of Cuito Cuanavale. The South Africans then went on the offensive and used artillery batteries to pound the town, destroying several military and government installations. UNITA infiltration teams also penetrated some areas of Cuito Cuanavale and sabotaged military infrastructures. Nevertheless, Angolan defenses in the town held. Cuban planes entered the battle, attacking South African ground positions. Without sufficient air cover, the South-African-UNITA forces disengaged from Cuito Cuanavale and withdrew to their bases in southern Angola.

The following year, 1987, massive shipments of Soviet arsenal arrived in Angola; these included 150 battle tanks; hundreds of armored carriers, trucks, and artillery pieces; and several planes and helicopters. In June, South African reconnaissance planes detected the movement of these Soviet weapons to Cuito Cuanavale. To the South Africans, the arms build-up meant that the Angolans were preparing for another large-scale offensive.

In July 1987, five Angolan brigades, supported by Cuban auxiliary units, advanced toward Mavinga. As in the previous campaigns, these forces were led by a Russian general. Opposition was overcome easily as UNITA units were forced back and came very close to being annihilated. The South Africans stepped in and, in a number of surprise counterattacks that included stopping the Angolan Army's attempt to cross the strategic Lomba River, succeeded in bringing the Angolan-Cuban offensive to a halt. Facing mounting losses in men and material, the Angolan-Cuban forces retreated to Cuito Cuanavale.

The South African-UNITA forces went on the offensive. After cutting off the approaches to Cuito Cuanavale, by November 1987, they had trapped the Angolans and Cubans in the town. The South Africans' long-range artillery batteries opened fire on Cuito Cuanavale, starting a barrage that lasted for two months.

After the South African-UNITA forces surrounded Cuito Cuanavale, the Angolan government appealed to Cuba for immediate assistance. As he had done in the Angolan War of Independence twelve years earlier, Fidel Castro, Cuba's leader, dispatched Cuban elite forces, as well as hundreds of tanks, armored transports, artillery pieces, and anti-aircraft weapons, and several planes. Some 55,000 Cuban soldiers soon arrived in Angola, with 40,000 sent to the front lines immediately. The arrival of Cuban troops and weapons at Cuito Cuanavale ended the South Africans' siege of the town.

Then in January 1988, in what was the first of many attempts, South African ground units, supported by UNITA auxiliaries attacked Cuito Cuanavale. The attack made some progress, but failed to break the town's defenses, and soon was called off. A second attempt was made in February, which nearly destroyed an Angolan Army brigade. But the Angolans managed to escape, forcing the South Africans to turn back. The next series of South African offensives, the last carried out in May 1987, met increasing resistance, as the battle lines consolidated. Finally, the South Africans abandoned their plan to capture Cuito Cuanavale and withdrew their forces, leaving behind their artillery batteries that continued to pound the town from long distance.

The South Africans' withdrawal ended the "Battle of Cuito Cuanavale", which actually consisted of several armed clashes from July 1987 to March 1988, and was the largest battle in Africa since the Battle of El Alamein in World War II. At Cuito Cuanavale, some 10,000 combatants from both sides were killed, while several thousands civilians died in the crossfire. Material losses were also extensive: hundreds of tanks, armored carriers, trucks, and other vehicles were lost or destroyed, as were several planes and helicopters.

After staving off defeat at Cuito Cuanavale, the Cubans opened another front in March 1988 in Angola's southwest, aimed directly at the South African stronghold of southern Cunene Province. Protected by Cuban planes, Cuban-Angolan armored and infantry units began advancing from Lubango, some 400 kilometers from the southern border. In a number of tit-for-tat clashes from May to June, the strength of the numerically superior Cuban-Angolan units forced the South Africans to yield ground steadily.

By June 1988, the Cuban-Angolan forces had advanced 300 kilometers, wresting control of the South African bases of Xangongo and Ongiva and coming to within striking distance of the Cunene River Hydroelectric Dam complex. The Cuban Air Force took control of the sky, as its modern Soviet-made planes and ground air-defense systems overwhelmed the obsolete aircraft of the South Africans. The Cubans established airbases in Cahama and Xangongo, some 100 kilometers from the border, where their planes projected into South-West Africa.

The Cuban-Angolan forces had gained the initiative in the war. By late June, the South Africans had retreated from Cunene Province into defensive lines in northern South-West Africa. In UNITA-held Cuando Cubango Province, South African units desisted from engaging in more battles. Angolan forces secured Cunene Province as large-scale fighting began to cease across the front lines.

Over the past years, the international community had tried in vain to bring the warring sides to the negotiating table. But with the heavy toll in human lives during the 1987 fighting, the combatants were determined to seek a permanent solution to the war. Moreover, the global political climate was changing. Starting in the mid-1980s, Soviet leader Mikhail Gorbachev implemented democratic and economic reforms in the USSR. Consequently, the United States and the Soviet Union moved toward improving diplomatic relations and the end of their Cold War. The two superpowers also ended support for their proxy armies around the world.

Cuba had for so long been denied by the United States to join the negotiations on the Angolan conflict. In peace talks held in January 1988, however, Cuban representatives were for the first time allowed to participate. Furthermore, South Africa had been reluctant to join the negotiations because of its security concerns. Two months after Cuba entered the negotiations, South Africa joined as well. Then in July, with American mediation, the negotiators agreed to the following: first, South Africa would withdraw its forces from Angola and South-West Africa; second, Cuba would also withdraw its forces from Angola; and third, South-West Africa would be granted independence.

In December 1988, a definitive peace agreement was signed in New York City, which essentially reaffirmed the agreement made in the July meetings. Earlier in August, South Africa had completed the withdrawal of its troops from Angola. Cuban troops withdrew in stages, with the last units leaving Angola in March 1991. The compliance of the peace agreement was overseen by a UN mission that had arrived in Angola. In March 1990, South-West Africa gained its independence as the Republic of Namibia.

In Angola itself, fighting between government troops and UNITA fighters restarted after the foreign troops withdrew from the country. A June 1989 ceasefire agreement between the two sides failed to hold as skirmishes broke out the following month. Attempts by other African countries to mediate a peace agreement also did not succeed. The government's Marxist stance and UNITA's democratic leanings appeared irreconcilable.

By the early 1990s, however, the Cold War had ended. Then in March 1991, Angola dropped communism and moved to adopt democracy. Urged on by Portugal (Angola's former colonial owner), the Angolan government and UNITA entered into peace negotiations in Bicesse, Portugal in May 1991. These negotiations bore fruit, as Angolan president Jose Eduardo dos Santos and UNITA leader Savimbi agreed to sign what became known as the Bicesse Accords, which carried a number of provisions including, a democratic government for Angola, a new national constitution, multi-party elections, and the integration of rebel fighters into the Angolan Armed Forces.

In September 1993, Angola held general elections. President dos Santos won the presidential race, gaining 49% of the votes against Savimbi's 40% – the remaining 11% was divided among the other presidential candidates (which included Holden Roberto of the FNLA or National Front for the Liberation of Angola; the FNLA was a rival nationalist movement of the MPLA during the Angolan War of Independence *(previous article)*, but became a political party after Angola transitioned to democracy).

UNITA and other political parties accused President dos Santos of cheating to win the presidency. Tensions resurfaced between the government and UNITA, which increased as both sides postured aggressively and hinted at a return to war. Armed clashes broke out in Luanda, which spread to other parts of the country. Then, in a three-day period between October 31 and November 2, 1992 in what is known as the "Halloween Massacre", the Angolan Army and pro-government vigilante groups attacked UNITA and FNLA supporters in Luanda. Some 10,000 to perhaps as many as 25,000 to 40,000 were killed; another 180,000 lost their lives during the next several months as the conflict escalated.

All-out war soon broke out. UNITA quickly gained control of 60% of the country, including capturing the cities of Caxito, Huambo, M'banza, Kongo, Ndalantado, and Uige. However, over the next several months, government forces launched counter-offensives that wrested back control of many rebel-captured areas. The insurgency was weakened seriously when the UN imposed a ban on arms sales to UNITA. Moreover, the United States, which was UNITA's long-time sympathizer, condemned Savimbi for restarting the war, and recognized the legitimacy of the Angolan government.

These military and diplomatic defeats forced Savimbi to sue for peace. Representatives of the Angolan government and UNITA met at Lusaka, Zambia, which led to the signing of another peace agreement, called the Lusaka Agreement, on October 31, 1994. This agreement carried some of the same provisions found in the 1991 Bicesse Accords, i.e. the end of the civil war, national reconciliation, and political and military integration. The UN force that already was present in Angola was tasked to monitor compliance to the Lusaka Agreement.

To show its genuine desire at reconciliation, the Angolan government appointed UNITA officials to national administrative posts, as well as to regional and local elective positions. Mediated by foreign countries, the government and UNITA held high-profile meetings in March 1996 to work out a power-sharing government. These meetings led to the formation of a coalition government called the "Government of Unity and National Reconciliation".

Despite outward appearances, however, distrust and hostility remained. In August 1996, Savimbi turned down President dos

Santos' offer of the vice-presidency. More crucially, both sides of the conflict were increasing their war stockpiles, with the government using its oil revenues, and UNITA using its sales of mined diamonds in its areas of control, to purchase weapons through covert sources, mainly in Eastern Europe. The Angolan government then announced that only a complete military victory could end the war.

In late 1998, fighting broke out. UNITA's capacity to wage war was weakened severely when the United Nations Security Council released two resolutions: a freeze on UNITA's bank accounts, and greater scrutiny of Angolan diamond sales transactions. Furthermore, UNITA's top leadership was wracked with dissent, leading to the formation of a break-away faction in September 1998. More dissident factions were formed in succeeding years. Militarily, too, UNITA was weakening, as government offensives captured large sections of rebel-held territory as well as huge stockpiles of weapons and ammunitions. UNITA's combat capability soon was reduced to using hit-and-run guerilla warfare.

Then in February 2002, Savimbi was killed by government forces. The rebel leader's death sparked a dramatic shift in Angola's security climate as the nearly three-decades' civil war suddenly came to an end. The government opened peace talks with UNITA leaders, which led to the rebels agreeing to lay down their weapons and return to the fold of the law.

A ceasefire was signed in April 2002. Five months later, in August, UNITA abolished its armed wing and demobilized its militia, and announced its transformation into an Angolan political party. It has since fielded candidates in elections, and constitutes the second-largest political party in the country.

The Angolan Civil War claimed some 500,000 human lives. Over four million Angolans (20% of the population) were displaced internally or fled as refugees to neighboring countries. This massive displacement of people caused a serious humanitarian crisis and a large pouring of international aid to Angola after the war. The war devastated the country, with the economy nearly insolvent, industries and infrastructures destroyed, and the people reeling in poverty.

Cabinda Secession When dealing with the two protracted wars that plagued Angola during the second half of the twentieth century (i.e. the "Angolan War of Independence" *(previous article)*, and the "Angolan Civil War"), discussion also must be made to the region of Cabinda, an Angolan Province that is physically separated from the rest of the country by a forty-kilometer strip of land belonging to the Democratic Republic of the Congo (Map 21).

Together with the Angolan nationalists that fought during the Angolan War of Independence, Cabindan nationalists under the Front for the Liberation of the Enclave of Cabinda (FLEC) sought the independence of Cabinda as a separate country from Angola. Portugal had administered Cabinda as part of Angola.

In August 1975, as the Portuguese were in the process of decolonizing from their African possessions, FLEC declared Cabinda's independence. Two months later, however, MPLA forces from Angola invaded Cabinda. On November 11, 1975, Angola became an independent state. Believing the new country to be the successor of the former colony of Angola, the Angolan government declared Cabinda as falling within the territorial jurisdiction of Angola. By early 1976, the MPLA had established a regional government in Cabinda and had gained control of the province's more populated areas. FLEC was pushed into the interior, where it has since engaged in a guerilla war of independence for nearly forty years.

The Cabindan people consider themselves to be culturally different from other Angolan ethnic groups and cite this reason as to why they should be allowed to form a separate state. In turn, Angola refuses to allow Cabinda to secede, not least because of Cabinda's large offshore oil reserves and oil revenues which account for 60% of all Angola's petrochemical production and constitute the country's main source of income.

UNITED STATES OCCUPATION OF NICARAGUA, 1912-1933

Nicaragua gained its independence in 1825 and thereafter experienced political instability for the rest of the nineteenth and into the twentieth centuries. The unrest resulted from the hostile relationship between Nicaragua's two political parties, the Conservatives and the Liberals, which often led to armed clashes, coups, and even civil wars. Nicaragua's instability was always a concern for the United States, because of American political and commercial interests in Nicaragua and other Central American countries (Map 22 shows Nicaragua and the other countries of Central America).

In many instances, Nicaragua's political troubles prompted American intervention, such as those that occurred in 1847, 1894, 1896, 1898, and 1899, when U.S. forces were landed in that Central American country. These occupations were brief, with American troops withdrawing once order had been restored, although U.S. Navy ships kept a permanent watch throughout the Central American coastline. The officially stated reasons given by the United States for intervening in Nicaragua was to protect American lives and American commercial interests in Central America. In some cases, however, the Americans wanted to give a decided advantage to one side of Nicaragua's political conflict.

In 1912, the United States again intervened in Nicaragua, starting an occupation of the country that would last for over two decades and would leave a deep impact on the local population. The origin of the 1912 American occupation traces back to the early 1900s when

Nicaragua, then led by the Liberals, offered the construction of the Nicaragua Canal to Germany and Japan. The Nicaragua Canal was planned to be a shipping waterway that connects the Pacific Ocean and the Atlantic Ocean through the Caribbean Sea.

The Liberals wanted less American involvement in Nicaragua's internal affairs and therefore offered the waterway's construction to other countries. Furthermore, the United States had decided to forgo its original plan to build the Nicaragua Canal in favor of completing the partly-finished Panama Canal (which had been abandoned by a French construction firm).

For the United States, however, the idea of another foreign power in the Western Hemisphere was anathema, as the U.S. government believed it had the exclusive rights to the region. The American policy of exclusivity in the Western Hemisphere was known as the Monroe Doctrine, set forth in 1823 by former U.S. president James Monroe. Furthermore, the United States believed that Nicaragua had ambitions in Central America and therefore viewed that country as a potential source of a wider conflict. U.S.-Nicaraguan relations deteriorated when two American saboteurs were executed by the Nicaraguan government. Consequently, the United States broke off diplomatic relations with Nicaragua.

In October 1909, Nicaraguan Conservatives, backed by some Liberals, carried out a rebellion against the government. The United States threw its support behind the rebels. Then when the rebellion spread, the United States sent warships to Nicaragua and subsequently, in December 1909, landed troops in Corinto and Bluefields (Map 23). More American forces arrived in May 1910.

In August 1910, Nicaragua's ruling government collapsed, replaced by a U.S.-friendly administration consisting of Conservatives and Liberals. The United States bought out Nicaragua's large foreign debt that had accumulated during the long period of instability. Consequently, Nicaragua owed the United States the amount of that debt, while the Americans' stake was raised in that troubled country.

Map 22. Central America: Belize, Guatemala, Honduras, El Salvador, Nicaragua, Costa Rica, and Panama. Mexico, on the north, forms part of North America, while Colombia, on the south and east, belongs to South America.

Then in 1912, Nicaragua's ruling coalition broke down, sparking a civil war between the government and another alliance of Liberals and Conservatives. As the rebels gained ground and began to threaten Managua, Nicaragua's capital, the United States landed troops in Corinto, Bluefields, and San Juan del Sur. At its peak, the U.S. troop deployment in Nicaragua totaled over 2,300 soldiers. Within a month of the deployment, in October 1912, the American troops, supported by Nicaraguan government forces, had defeated the rebels.

The United States tightened its control of Nicaragua in August 1914 when both countries signed an agreement whereby the Americans gained exclusive rights to construct the Nicaragua Canal, as well as to establish military bases to protect it. The U.S.-Nicaragua treaty mostly served as a deterrent against other foreign involvement in Nicaragua, since by this time, the Americans already were operating the Panama Canal nearby.

The U.S. Army's presence in Nicaragua from 1912 to 1925 brought peace in that Central American country. At the Nicaraguan government's request, the U.S. Army helped to organize Nicaragua's armed forces and police forces (collectively called the National Guard) to eliminate the many private militias and other armed groups that local politicians were using to advance their personal interests. After the National Guard was formed, the United States withdrew its forces from Nicaragua. Nine months later, however, in-fighting among Conservatives led to the overthrow of the incumbent president, again prompting the United States to redeploy its military forces in Nicaragua to stop the disturbance from spreading.

Peace and order was restored once more, and a new Conservative government came to power. The Conservatives' authority was challenged by the Liberals, however, who formed their own government. Fighting soon broke out between the rival political parties, which rapidly escalated into a civil war. Once more, the United States intervened and restored peace after threatening to use military force against the Liberals. In the peace treaty that followed, the Conservatives and Liberals agreed to two stipulations: that the Conservative government would complete its term of office before new elections were held; and that all remaining private militias and armed groups would be disbanded and subsequently incorporated into the government forces to form an expanded, non-partisan National Guard.

Map 23. Nicaragua. The U.S. decision to invade Nicaragua in 1912 was due, at least in part, to the American government's concern that another foreign power would build and then control the Nicaragua Canal. The United States regarded the whole Western Hemisphere as its exclusive sphere of influence. The Nicaragua Canal was intended to be a shipping waterway that connects the Pacific Ocean and Caribbean Sea.

All armed groups complied with the peace agreement, except for an obscure pro-Liberal militia led by Augusto Sandino, who continued to oppose the authority of the Conservative government. Sandino also condemned the National Guard, which he believed was being used by the United States to meddle into Nicaragua's internal affairs. From

1927 to 1932, Sandino carried out a guerilla war against the Nicaraguan and American forces, successfully evading capture and gaining the support of the rural people through his calls for both the end of foreign control of the country and the local elite's social and economic domination of Nicaraguan society.

In 1933, the United States withdrew its forces from Nicaragua because of budgetary constraints from the ongoing Great Depression. The American public's opposition to the Nicaraguan occupation, as well as mounting soldier casualties, also factored into the U.S. government's decision to withdraw from that Central American country.

In Nicaragua, Anastacio Somoza, who led the National Guard, gained considerable influence during the early 1930s. Then in 1934, he ordered the assassination of Sandino, who had begun peace talks with the Nicaraguan government after the American troops departed from the country. Sandino was killed by members of the National Guard in February 1934 in Managua. Through political manipulations, Somoza installed his close friends and allies to high-level government positions and subsequently forced Nicaragua's president to resign from office in 1936. A year later, Somoza became Nicaragua's president, starting a dictatorship, a repressive regime, and a political dynasty that lasted over forty years. In 1979, an insurgent group called the Sandinistas, who invoked the ideas of Sandino, ended the Somoza dynasty after overthrowing the dictator's son, who was Nicaragua's president by then *(next article)*.

NICARAGUAN REVOLUTION (1961 - 1979) AND COUNTER-REVOLUTION (1981 - 1990)

Revolution In 1961, the revolutionary movement called the Sandinista National Liberation Front was formed in Nicaragua with two main objectives: to end the U.S.-backed Somoza regime, and establish a socialist government in the country. The movement and its members, who were called Sandinistas, took their name and ideals from Augusto Sandino, a Nicaraguan rebel fighter of the 1930s, who fought a guerilla war against the American forces that had invaded and occupied Nicaragua. Sandino also wanted to end the Nicaraguan wealthy elite's stranglehold on society. He advocated for social justice and economic equality for all Nicaraguans.

By the late 1970s, Nicaragua had been ruled for over forty years by the Somoza family in a dynastic-type succession that had begun in the 1930s. In 1936, Anastacio Somoza seized power in Nicaragua and gained total control of all aspects of the government. Officially, he was the country's president, but ruled as a dictator. Over time, President Somoza accumulated great wealth and owned the biggest landholdings in the country. His many personal and family businesses extended into the shipping and airlines industries, agricultural plantations and cattle ranches, sugar mills, and wine manufacturing. President Somoza took bribes from foreign corporations that he had granted mining concessions in the country, and also benefited from local illicit operations such as unregistered gambling, organized prostitution, and illegal wine production.

President Somoza suppressed all forms of opposition with the use of the National Guard, Nicaragua's police force, which had turned the country into a militarized state. President Somoza was staunchly anti-communist and received strong military and financial support from the United States, which was willing to take Nicaragua's repressive government as an ally in the ongoing Cold War.

In 1956, President Somoza was assassinated and was succeeded by his son, Luis, who also ruled as a dictator until his own death by heart failure in 1967. In turn, Luis was succeeded by his younger brother, Anastacio Somoza, who had the same first name as their father. As Nicaragua's new head of state, President Somoza outright established a harsh regime much like his father had in the 1930s. Consequently, the Sandinistas intensified their militant activities in the rural areas, mainly in northern Nicaragua. Small bands of Sandinistas carried out guerilla operations, such as raiding isolated army outposts and destroying government facilities.

By the early 1970s, the Sandinistas comprised only a small militia in contrast to Nicaragua's U.S.-backed National Guard. The Sandinistas struck great fear on President Somoza, however, because of the rebels' symbolic association to Sandino. President Somoza wanted to destroy the Sandinistas with a passion that bordered on paranoia. He ordered his forces to the countryside to hunt down and kill Sandinistas. These military operations greatly affected the rural population, however, who began to fear as well as hate the government.

The end of the Somoza regime began in 1972 when a powerful earthquake hit Managua, Nicaragua's capital. The destruction resulting from the earthquake caused 5,000 human deaths and 20,000 wounded, and left half a million people homeless (nearly half of Managua's population). Managua was devastated almost completely, cutting off all government services. In the midst of the destruction, however,

President Somoza diverted the international relief money to his personal bank account, greatly reducing the government's meager resources. Consequently, thousands of people were deprived of food, clothing, and shelter.

Business owners in Managua also were affected by the earthquake and railed at the government's corruption and ineptitude to deal with the tragedy. Consequently, many businesses closed, causing many workers to lose their jobs and worsen the country's dire unemployment situation. Nicaragua's political opposition, which formed a broad spectrum from the far left to the moderate right, became much more vocal in its criticism of the government. For the opposition, the Sandinistas' overthrow of President Somoza did not seem as repugnant as before.

In December 1974, Sandinista rebels took hostage a number of high-ranking government officials, including some of President Somoza's relatives. After negotiations were held between the government and the rebels, President Somoza agreed to pay a large ransom for the hostages' release. Furthermore, President Somoza was forced to free a number of jailed Sandinistas. The success of the hostage taking greatly raised the people's perception of the Sandinistas and also shattered the purported invincibility of President Somoza.

President Somoza retaliated by imposing a state of siege across the country. He ordered the National Guard to conduct a campaign of terror in the countryside. Consequently, the military committed many atrocities against rural civilians. As Nicaragua's human rights situation deteriorated, U.S. president Jimmy Carter exerted diplomatic pressure on the Somoza regime. With President Somoza continuing his repressive policies, however, the U.S. government suspended military assistance to Nicaragua in February 1978.

Later in the year, Sandinista fighters seized Nicaragua's National Legislature and took hostage hundreds of lawmakers and high-ranking government officials. Once again, President Somoza was forced to negotiate and then yield to the rebels' demands that included paying a big ransom for the hostages' release and freeing more political prisoners.

Nicaragua's opposition parties united and tried to negotiate with the national government. By the end of 1978, however, President Somoza's intransigence had led many in the political opposition to lose hope for a peaceful solution to the country's political crisis.

In early 1979, the Sandinistas succeeded in reuniting rival factions after experiencing a power struggle that nearly broke the organization. The Sandinistas formed an alliance with and subsequently led a coalition of opposition parties that included communists, socialists, Liberals, Conservatives, and centrists.

The Sandinistas received weapons from Cuba, Venezuela, and Panama. Then in March 1977, from their bases in northern Nicaragua and in Costa Rica, the Sandinistas launched more potent attacks against National Guard units (Map 24). By early June 1979, the Sandinistas had captured the whole northern section of the country. On June 16, the strategic city of Leon fell to the rebels. On June 20, the United States broke off diplomatic relations with the Somoza regime following the brazen killing of an American news reporter by a Nicaraguan soldier. The assault on the American journalist was caught on live TV, generating outrage and condemnation from the American people.

By early July 1979, the Sandinistas had surrounded Managua; the rest of the country had already fallen into their hands. With his government on the brink of collapse, President Somoza fled from the country on July 17. His assassination by Sandinista commandos in

Paraguay the following year completed the full turn-around of the Somoza-Sandino saga.

On July 19, 1979, Sandinista forces entered Managua where huge crowds welcomed them as liberators. Following President Somoza's overthrow, a civilian junta that had been set up earlier by the opposition coalition began to rule the country. The junta represented a cross-section of the political opposition and was structured as a power-sharing government.

Map 24. Nicaraguan Revolution (1961-1979). Communist rebels called Sandinistas fought to overthrow the autocratic regime of Anastacio Somoza. The Somoza dynasty ended when the rebels captured Managua, Nicaragua's capital.

Non-Sandinista members of the junta soon resigned, however, as they felt powerless against the Sandinistas (who effectively controlled the junta) and feared that the government was moving toward adopting Cuban-style socialism.

By 1980, the Sandinistas had taken full control of the government. The country had been devastated by the war, as well as by the corruption and neglect by the previous dictatorial regimes. Using the limited resources available, the Sandinista government launched many programs for the general population. The most successful of these programs were in public education, where the country's high illiteracy rate was lowered significantly, and in agrarian reform, where large landholdings, including those of ex-President Somoza, were seized and distributed to the peasants and poor farmers. The Sandinista government also implemented programs in health care, the arts and culture, and in the labor sector.

U.S. president Carter was receptive to the Sandinista government. But President Ronald Reagan, who succeeded as U.S. head of state in January 1981, was alarmed that Nicaragua had allowed a communist toehold in the American continental mainland, and therefore posed a threat to the United States. President Reagan believed that the Sandinistas planned to spread communism across Central America. As evidence of this perception, President Reagan pointed out that the Sandinistas were arming the communist insurgents in El Salvador. Consequently, President Reagan prepared plans for a counter-revolution in Nicaragua that would overthrow the Sandinista government.

Counter-Revolution President Reagan cut off financial assistance to Nicaragua in January 1981 (his first month as president) in order to undermine the Sandinista government. Then in the summer through autumn of 1981, the Central Intelligence Agency (CIA) formed an armed militia consisting of remnants of Nicaragua's former National

Guard who had fled to Honduras after President Somoza's overthrow. The CIA subsequently also organized other anti-Sandinista militias based in Honduras and Costa Rica. These CIA-backed militias collectively were called "Contras" which was shortened from the Spanish word *"contrarevolution"*, or counter-revolution. The Contras' principal aim was to overthrow the Sandinista government.

The Contras were most active in the northern, central, and western regions of the country. Operating in western Nicaragua were small Contra militias composed of local indigenous peoples who opposed the government's expropriation of their ancestral lands. Another Contra militia led by an ex-Sandinista commander fought out of the Rio San Juan region.

The Contra War, as the conflict was known, did not threaten seriously the Sandinista regime, but it devastated much of the country, especially in the rural areas. The United States, supported by other Western countries, imposed an arms embargo on Nicaragua, forcing the Sandinista government to purchase weapons from the Soviet Union. Because of the Contra insurgency, the Nicaraguan government tried to force military conscription. The civilian population resisted fiercely, however, with riots and protests breaking out in some areas. The war devastated Nicaragua's economy, particularly in regions affected by the fighting. Furthermore, the United States, which purchased 90% of Nicaragua's exports, imposed a trade embargo against that Central American country.

The Contras committed many atrocities against civilians: summary executions, tortures, rapes, lootings, and arson occurred frequently during the war. When reports of these atrocities reached the United States, the U.S. Congress, in 1985, cut off funding to the Contras. Other factors that influenced the U.S. Congress' decision were: the American public generally was not sympathetic to the Contras; the CIA was implicated in the mining of Nicaraguan ports; President Reagan's surreptitious conduct of the war; and the minor involvement of the Soviet Union in the war, despite contrary claims by the U.S. government.

The Reagan administration was determined to continue supporting the Contras despite the U.S. Congress legislation. The CIA and the National Security Council (NSC) devised a plan whereby American weapons were sold secretly to Iran (which was then embroiled in a bitter war with Iraq called the "Iran-Iraq War"). The proceeds from the weapons' sales were then used to fund the Contras. American authorities discovered the scheme, however, leading to an investigation by U.S. Congress. Consequently, government officials in the Reagan administration were implicated. Further damning U.S. involvement were allegations that the CIA trafficked illegal narcotics from Central America to the United States and then used the proceeds from the drugs' sales to fund the Contras.

Meanwhile in Nicaragua, bitter fighting occurred in the Zelaya Provinces in December 1987 and near the Honduran border in March 1988. The war was going nowhere, however, with human casualties topping 40,000 and rising daily. The Contras were demoralized and suffered desertions because of their failure to win territories, diminished U.S. funding, and corruption of their leaders. The Sandinista government also was weary from the decades of war; it also faced a restive population that longed for peace.

In an earlier meeting held in Guatemala in August 1987, the leaders of Central American countries had agreed to work together to bring about peace in the region and in their respective troubled countries (i.e. the leftist insurgencies in Guatemala and El Salvador, the military dictatorship in Panama, a right-wing insurgency in Nicaragua, and political unrest in Honduras). In March 1988, Contra rebels agreed to hold peace talks with the Nicaraguan government, despite fierce opposition by the Reagan administration. Subsequently, a ceasefire was agreed, pending Nicaragua's return to democracy and the holding of free elections.

Then in general elections held in February 1990, the Sandinistas lost control of the government in a stunning defeat. A new government was formed consisting of a broad coalition of many opposition political parties. Consequently, the Contras voluntarily laid down their weapons and returned to the fold of the law. Nicaragua's three decades of war finally came to an end.

FOOTBALL WAR

In July 1969, El Salvador and Honduras fought a brief, emotionally charged war only two weeks after their soccer teams had played a series of qualifying matches for the 1970 FIFA (Fédération Internationale de Football Association) World Cup. The intense displays of nationalism from both sides, coupled with the widespread violence during the games, triggered the outbreak of the war. Nevertheless, the underlying causes of the war were much more complex.

Background During the 1920s, El Salvador experienced great social and economic stresses resulting from the following factors: the loss of agricultural lands to wealthy plantation owners, the country's diminishing natural resources, high levels of unemployment, and a rapid population growth. As a result, many Salvadorans crossed the border into neighboring Honduras, which was less densely populated, largely undeveloped, and much more spacious, as it was five times bigger than El Salvador. The influx of Salvadorans into Honduras continued for the next forty years and progressively spread further inland.

By the 1960s, Salvadorans constituted 10% of Honduras' population and 20% of its work force, with their livelihoods as diverse as subsidence farmers, farm and industry workers, and even shop owners in towns and cities. More critically, Salvadoran farmers did not register their lands nor did Salvadorans in general acquire Honduran citizenship, making them undocumented foreigners in Honduras.

Initially, Honduras' vast frontier readily absorbed the large Salvadoran influx. Furthermore, Honduras' border with El Salvador was porous and improperly demarcated ever since the two countries gained their independences in the 1840s. Honduras and El Salvador had signed a number of treaties intended to regulate human traffic into each other's territories, but these were not implemented strictly.

Then in 1966, large corporations in the Honduran agricultural industry called upon the government to ensure the rights of Hondurans to their lands. These corporations also accused Salvadoran farmers of illegally possessing Honduran lands. Consequently, an anti-Salvadoran sentiment developed among the Honduran population.

The anti-Salvadoran sentiment presented the Honduran government the perfect opportunity to deflect away from Honduras' economic and labor problems and instead fault the Salvadoran immigrants for all the country's ills. Adding to the Hondurans' anti-Salvadoran sentiment was El Salvador's much higher economic productivity compared to Honduras. And within the Central American Common Market, the region's trade organization, El Salvador was a net exporter of commodities while Honduras bought more goods than it sold.

During the 1960s, Honduras passed an agrarian reform law to support its agricultural modernization and export diversification programs. The land reform law limited ownership of Honduran land to native-born citizens, thereby denying the Salvadoran immigrants of all rights to their lands and farms. In January 1969, Honduras did not renew the 1967 Bilateral Treaty with El Salvador, thereby making it illegal for undocumented Salvadorans to enter Honduras.

By May 1969, the land reform law in Honduras was being fully implemented. Thousands of dispossessed Salvadoran families returned to El Salvador, causing a sudden surge in the Salvadoran population, and straining the country's economic resources and the government's capacity to provide public services. El Salvador condemned Honduras, generating tensions and animosity on both sides. Nationalistic sentiments were fueled by propaganda and rhetoric spouted by the media from the two sides.

Such was the charged atmosphere leading up to the three football matches between El Salvador and Honduras in June 1969. The first match was played on June 8 in Tegucigalpa, Honduras' capital, which was won by the host team. Aside from some fans fighting in the stands, no major security breakdown occurred during the match.

In El Salvador, however, soccer fans were infuriated by the result, believing they had been cheated. The Salvadoran media described the football matches as epitomizing the "national honor". After the defeat, a despondent Salvadoran fan died after shooting herself. Her death became a rallying cry for Salvadorans who considered her a martyr. Thousands of Salvadorans, including the country's president and other top government officials, attended her funeral and joined the nation in mourning her death.

The second match was played in El Salvador, and was won also by the home team, thereby leveling the series at one win apiece. The tense situation during the game broke out in widespread violence across the capital, San Salvador. Street clashes led to many deaths, including those of Honduran fans. As a precaution, the Honduran football team was housed in an undisclosed location and driven to the game in armored vehicles. After the game, the Honduran team's vehicles plying the road back to Honduras were stoned while passing through Salvadoran towns.

In Honduras, the people retaliated by attacking and looting Salvadoran shops in Tegucigalpa and other cities and towns. Armed bands of thugs roamed the countryside targeting Salvadorans – beating up and killing men, raping women, burning houses, and destroying farms. Thousands of Salvadorans fled toward the border to El

Salvador. And as the prospect of war drew closer, Salvadoran and Honduran security forces guarding the border engaged in sporadic exchanges of gunfire.

The third, deciding football match was played on June 26 in Mexico City, which was won by the Salvadoran team. Two days earlier, Honduras had cut diplomatic relations with El Salvador. The Salvadoran government reciprocated on June 26, accusing Honduras of committing "genocide" by killing Salvadoran immigrants. The two sides prepared for war by increasing their weapons stockpiles, which were sourced from private dealers because the United States had imposed an arms embargo.

War On July 3 and July 14, Honduran planes flew over Salvadoran air space. El Salvador condemned the territorial violations and sprung into military action. In the afternoon of July 14, Salvadoran aircraft, including C-47 transports that were improvised to dispense bombs, attacked Honduran airfields in Tegucigalpa and other locations. The Salvadoran objective was a pre-emptive air strike to destroy the much larger Honduran Air Force on the ground. However, no significant damage was made on the Honduran planes.

A few hours later and under cover of evening darkness, Salvadoran ground forces crossed the border into Honduras (Map 25). Major Salvadoran offensives were made in Honduras' eastern province of Valle, leading to the capture of the towns of Aramecina and Goascoran, and in Ocotepeque Province in the west, where Nueva Ocotepeque and La Labor were taken. The Salvadoran Army also captured Honduras' north central border towns of Guarita, Valladolid, and La Virtud, and the Honduran islands in the Gulf of Fonseca, off the Pacific coast.

By the second day of the invasion, July 15, Salvadoran forces had penetrated eight kilometers inside Honduras and were threatening

Tegucigalpa via the main road. Honduran resistance increased as thousands of civilian volunteers, who had been given weapons by the government, joined the Honduran Army in battle.

Honduran warplanes attacked Salvadoran air bases, destroying many planes. The Honduran airstrikes also targeted Salvadoran port facilities and oil refineries. The Honduran Air Force gained mastery of the sky. With the destruction of several of its oil storage facilities, El Salvador experienced fuel shortages that severely crippled its capacity to transport troops and supplies to the front lines. By the third day, the Salvadoran offensive had ground to a halt.

Map 25. Football War. In 1969, El Salvador launched military operations inside Honduras. The areas affected by the war are indicated.

At the onset of the war, the Organization of American States, or OAS, had tried to impose a ceasefire. El Salvador had resisted, as its forces were on the attack. But when its offensive bogged down, the Salvadoran government agreed to end hostilities, on July 18, four days after the war began (thus, another name of the war is the "Hundred Hours War"). A ceasefire took effect two days later.

In August 1969, after lengthy negotiations, El Salvador agreed to withdraw its forces from captured territories in Honduras. In return, the Honduran government promised to ensure the safety of the remaining Salvadoran residents in Honduras. OAS representatives arrived in Honduras to oversee compliance of the agreement by both sides.

Some 3,000 persons, mostly Honduran civilians, died in the war. In the period following the war, thousands of Salvadorans were dispossessed of their homes and livelihoods in Honduras, and eventually returned to El Salvador.

In October 1980, more than a decade after the war, El Salvador and Honduras signed a final peace agreement and raised the issue of their imprecise border to the International Court of Justice, or ICJ. The two countries agreed to respect the ICJ's decision. In October 1992, the ICJ awarded two-thirds of the undefined areas to Honduras and the rest (one-third) to El Salvador. A definite border also was established.

After the war, Honduras' economy declined because of the loss of Salvadoran labor, as well as by the loss of Salvadoran agricultural and industrial contributions to Honduran productivity. In El Salvador, the repercussions were even more severe: the spike in the Salvadoran population by the returnees caused a severe strain on the national economy. Unemployment and poverty rose. The severe social and economic stresses contributed greatly to the even more calamitous Salvadoran Civil War that broke out a decade later.

DIRTY WAR

The Dirty War refers to the Argentinean military government's suppression of left-wing and perceived communist elements during the mid-1970s to the early 1980s. The "Dirty" in its name refers to the violent, illicit methods used by the military to carry out the campaign. These "dirty" methods included summary executions, extrajudicial arrests and detentions, tortures, abductions, and rapes. The military justified these methods on the grounds that their enemies were using terrorism and other underhanded actions against the civilian population and even against the government itself. The Argentinean authorities also declared that drastic measures were needed as the country was falling into anarchy, a claim that was rejected by the political opposition. What is undisputed, however, was the presence of widespread violence and considerable tensions leading up to the Dirty War.

The origin of the Dirty War can be traced back to the rise of Juan Peron, Argentina's extremely popular president during the 1940s to the 1950s, and his politics of Peronism, a unique, all-inclusive nationalist ideology. Peronism gained broad support from the common people, workers, and peasants, as well as from the political left, moderates, and even the far-right. In 1955, however, President Peron was deposed in a military coup. Argentina then came under military rule, and Peronism and Peronist parties were banned.

By the late 1960s, the remaining Peronist movements had given way to various radical and communist armed groups that had sprung up as a result of Fidel Castro's communist victory in Cuba and the subsequent spread of Marxist ideology across Latin America. In the early 1970s, the Argentinean insurgents carried out attacks against civilian and military targets. Rebel actions included assassinations, summary killings, abductions, bombings, and armed robberies.

Partly because of the increasing civil unrest as well as an ailing economy, the Argentinean military government lifted the ban on Peronism. Then in elections held in May 1973, a left-wing Peronist political party came to power. The new government freed political prisoners and enacted pro-leftist laws. The resurgent labor union staged job actions, causing many businesses to close down. Many foreign investors left the country after receiving threats on their lives, businesses, and properties.

With the ban on his return lifted, ex-President Peron returned to Argentina in June 1973. But what should have been cause for celebration instead generated a fatal split in Peronism. Some two million Peronist supporters welcomed Peron on his arrival at the airport. When commotion broke out, however, Peron's armed right-wing supporters fired on the left-wing Peronists in the crowd, killing 13 persons and wounding over 300 others.

The following month, the left-wing Peronist government stepped down, giving way to Peron to take up the presidency, since he had won the presidential election held a few months earlier. President Peron's vice-president was Isabel Peron, his wife, who won the vice-presidential race. President Peron was supported by a broad political coalition and a massive populist base that included leftist elements. He cast his lot with his right-wing supporters, however, and formed a government composed of the bureaucratic elite, as well as some moderates.

By May 1974, President Peron had purged his government and political party of left-leaning politicians; his left-wing supporters at the lower echelons had been alienated as well. But already in failing health at age 78, President Peron's final term in office lasted only ten months, as he passed away on June 1, 1974.

Isabel Peron, the vice-president, succeeded as Argentina's new president. Isabel's political inexperience manifested, however, as she was incapable of confronting the country's many problems. High-ranking government and military leaders interfered constantly in major government policy decisions, and Isabel was reduced to a figurehead president.

Map 26. Argentina and nearby countries. During the Dirty War, the Argentine government used "dirty" methods in its anti-insurgency campaign to stamp out leftist and perceived communist elements in the country.

The growing influence of the military in Argentinean politics plunged the country deeper into the Dirty War, which actually had begun near the end of Juan Peron's presidency. Extremist right-wing politicians close to Juan Peron had organized the "Argentine Anti-Communist Alliance" or "Triple A", a clandestine state-run "death squad" that initially targeted union leaders, but expanded its operations to include all leftist elements, as well as political dissidents.

The Argentinean communists also militarized, terrorizing private businesses with bombings, arsons, and armed robberies, and kidnapping or killing businessmen, managers, and executives. The insurgents also attacked police stations and army outposts, causing hundreds of military and police casualties.

In 1975, the communist rebels gained a third section of Tucuman Province in Argentina's northwest region (Map 26). The government issued the so-called "Annihilation Decrees", which authorized the military to crush the insurgency. The country was reconfigured into military zones, greatly reducing the civilian government's authority.

In March 1976, high-ranking military officers deposed Isabel Peron. The military's stated reason for the coup was to prevent the communist take-over of the country. Thereafter, a military junta came to power. Argentina's legislature was abolished, while the judicial courts were restructured to suit the new militarized system. The academic and intelligentsia were suppressed, as were labor and peoples' assemblies. The military government instituted harsh measures to stamp out communist and leftist elements. Also targeted by the military were opposition politicians, journalists, writers, labor and student leaders, including their supporters and sympathizers.

The military operated with impunity, arbitrarily subjecting their suspected enemies to arrests, interrogations, tortures, and executions. One infamous method of execution was the "death flight", where prisoners were drugged, stripped naked, and held down with weights on their feet, and then boarded onto a plane and later thrown out into the Atlantic Ocean. Since death flights and other forms of executions made certain that the bodies would not be found, the victims were said to have disappeared, striking great fear among the people. Another atrocity was allowing captured pregnant women to give birth and then killing them, with their babies given to the care of and adopted by military or right-leaning couples. The military and Triple A death squads carried out these operations clandestinely during the Dirty War.

The military government's anti-insurgency campaign was so fierce, sustained, and effective that by 1977, the leftist and communist groups had practically ceased to exist. Hundreds of rebels, who had escaped to the nearby countries of Brazil, Uruguay, Paraguay, Bolivia, and Chile, were arrested and returned to Argentina. The United States provided technical assistance to the integrated intelligence network of these countries within the scope of its larger struggle against communism in the Cold War.

The Argentinean government continued its draconian rule even after it had stamped out the insurgency. The Dirty War caused some 9,000 confirmed and up to 30,000 unconfirmed victims from murders and forced disappearances. By 1982, however, the military's anti-insurgency campaign, which had found wide popular support initially, was being criticized by the people because of high-level government corruption and a floundering national economy.

Seeking to revitalize its flagging image, the military government launched an invasion of the British-controlled Falkland Islands in an attempt to stir up nationalist sentiments and thereby regain the Argentinean people's support. The Argentinean forces briefly gained control of the islands. A British naval task force soon arrived, however, and recaptured the Falkland Islands, driving away and inflicting heavy casualties on the Argentinean forces.

Consequently, Argentina's military government collapsed, ending the country's militarized climate. Argentina then began to transition to civilian rule under a democratic system. After the country held general elections in 1983, the new government that came to power opened a commission to investigate the crimes committed during the Dirty War. Subsequently, a number of perpetrators were brought to trial and convicted. Some military units broke out in rebellion in protest of the convictions, forcing the Argentinean government to pass new laws that reduced the military's liability during the Dirty War. In 1989, a broad amnesty was given to all persons who had been involved, indicted, and even convicted of crimes during the Dirty War.

In June 2005, however, the Argentinean Supreme Court overturned the amnesty laws, allowing for the re-opening of criminal lawsuits for Dirty War crimes. The fates of many persons killed and disappeared, as well as the infants taken from their murdered mothers, remain unsolved and are subject to ongoing investigations.

CHACO WAR

Background In the 1930s, Paraguay and Bolivia went to war for possession of the North Chaco, a dry, forbidding expanse of scrub and forest that lay between the two countries (Map 27). The North Chaco forms a part of the larger Gran Chaco Plains, a vast region that extends into northern Argentina, western Paraguay, eastern Bolivia, and a small section in western Brazil.

During the colonial era, the Gran Chaco Plains was administered by the Spanish government as a separate territory. In the early 1800s, the Gran Chaco Plains became disputed territory when the South American countries surrounding it gained their independences. The delineation of the borders around the Gran Chaco Plains was not pursued actively, however, because of the region's harsh climate and the mistaken belief that it contained few natural resources.

Through conquest from wars later in the 1800s, many areas of the Gran Chaco Plains were annexed by the victorious countries. Eventually, what remained undecided was the North Chaco, the region straddling Paraguay and Bolivia and located west of the Paraguay River and north of the Pilcomayo River.

Bolivia presented colonial-era documents purporting its ownership to the North Chaco. Paraguay, however, took an active, practical approach to acquire the region. For example, the Paraguayan government encouraged wealthy farmers to build ranches there. Paraguay also sold lands in the North Chaco to foreign investors, particularly Argentineans, and the Mennonites (a religious sect) from Europe and North America. Furthermore, the Guarani people, North Chaco's indigenous tribe, were ethnically and culturally related to the native Paraguayans. And Paraguay's other national language, apart from Spanish, was Guarani.

Paraguayans soon gained dominance in the North Chaco. Bolivians who settled there were met with varied responses from the Paraguayan government – from issuing weak diplomatic protests to violently evicting the Bolivian settlers. Representatives from Paraguay and Bolivia met a number of times to try to work out a common border, but these meetings failed to achieve anything substantial, as no reason existed to map out the seemingly worthless piece of land.

Then, oil was discovered at the foothills of the Andes Mountains, located in Bolivia's western end of the Chaco. Soon, a foreign oil company was producing commercial quantities of oil for Bolivia in the Andes foothills. Bolivia needed an outlet to the sea in order to export the oil. It had lost its only maritime access (through the Pacific Ocean) after its defeat in a war against Chile in the 1880s. Rather than risk another war against powerful Chile to regain its Pacific outlet, Bolivia turned to the North Chaco as a seemingly easier obstacle to gain access to the sea.

Bolivia believed that its large armed forces could easily overpower the much smaller Paraguayan Army. After it had achieved a military victory, Bolivia could then take control of the North Chaco, which it also believed contained oil deposits, as it lay adjacent to the Andes oil fields. And with the Paraguay River situated at the eastern end of the North Chaco, Bolivia would gain access to the Atlantic Ocean. This scenario was not lost to Paraguay. Backed by another foreign oil company, the Paraguayans also desired the North Chaco's potential oil wealth.

With foreign oil companies promising them huge profits, Paraguay and Bolivia pursued vigorous claims to the North Chaco. The region became militarized as both countries constructed army garrisons called "fortins" ("fortin" is a Spanish word that means "little fort") deep inside unoccupied areas. Fighting inevitably followed.

In February 1927, Bolivian forces captured a Paraguayan Army patrol, killing its commander. In December 1928, Paraguayan troops overran a Bolivian fortin. In response, Bolivia sent more troops to the North Chaco in order to seize Paraguayan outposts and harass Paraguayan settlements.

Map 27. North Chaco (shaded) was the scene of a territorial war between Paraguay and Bolivia in the 1930s.

The United States, which had a strong interest in Bolivia's oil industry, tried to exert diplomatic pressure on the two sides. Other countries, particularly Argentina and Belgium, as well as other Latin

American governments, tried to force a peaceful settlement. By the early 1930s, Paraguay and Bolivia were unyielding. And with the North Chaco now bristling with dozens of armed fortins, war was inevitable.

War The war began with two small encounters for control of Lake Pitiantuta (Map 28), which had been recently discovered by the Paraguayans and was mutually desired for its water in the otherwise semi-arid wasteland. The first of these encounters occurred in June 1932 when Bolivian forces overran the Paraguayan detachment at the lake. The following month, a large Paraguayan Army contingent drove away the Bolivians from the lake. The Bolivian government sent thousands of reinforcements to the North Chaco. A Bolivian offensive captured three Paraguayan outposts, including the strategic Fortin Boqueron, located inside the eastern third section of the North Chaco.

The Paraguayan government called for general mobilization, leading thousands of zealous Paraguayans to join the army. From a small force of 4,000 soldiers, the Paraguayan Armed Forces grew to 60,000 troops within a short time. The nationalistic zeal displayed among the army ranks extended to the top commanders, many of whom had fought in World War I and had learned much from that war's biter trench warfare.

Because of budgetary constraints, the Paraguayan government purchased only the cheaper weapons from international dealers. As it turned out, the purchases were propitious, as the weapons were light and ideally suited for portability in North Chaco's forbidding climate.

In battle, the Paraguayan forces refrained from engaging in direct frontal combat because of their limited resources in men and material. Instead, they fought in many small, highly mobile teams that penetrated, surrounded, and destroyed the much larger Bolivian Army units.

The North Chaco harbored diseases such as malaria and yellow fever, and was teeming with wild animals and legions of ferocious insects. These, together with the sweltering climate, afflicted both sides, but more so the Bolivian soldiers, 80% of whom were indigenous peoples from Bolivia's western highlands who fell victim to the elements much more than to the fighting itself. Furthermore, most of the Bolivian troops had been forced into military service and had neither interest in the war nor in their country itself, since Bolivia's government, led by the Spanish-descended elite, had long neglected and had yet to integrate the country's large indigenous population.

The ranks of the Bolivian Army were disciplined, but their commanders, who were led initially by a World War I veteran Germany Army officer, were incompetent. The Bolivian Army High Command used static defenses and unsupported frontal attacks, and ignored air reconnaissance information. Consequently, large, cumbersome Bolivian units were cut down to pieces by many swift, smaller Paraguayan Army teams. Furthermore, insufficient water supply to the Bolivians fighting at the front lines decided many battles; whole units surrendered when their water ran out, while separated Bolivian soldiers perished from thirst.

By August 1932, Paraguay had fully mobilized its forces. A Paraguayan offensive in September recaptured Fortin Boqueron and other smaller garrisons nearby. In December, Bolivia sent many troops and weapons to the North Chaco for a full-scale offensive aimed at taking the whole region and then advancing right up to Asuncion, Paraguay's capital. From January to March 1933, Bolivian offensives overran several Paraguayan fortifications. Then in a major battle at Fortin Nanawa, which was the Paraguayan Army's headquarters in the North Chaco, the Bolivians were stopped.

Nearly a year after the war began, Paraguay declared war on Bolivia. The Bolivians made preparations for another general offensive on Fortin Nanawa. After assembling a sizable force, the Bolivians attacked Fortin Nanawa in July but were repulsed again, with heavy Bolivian losses. The Bolivian offensives in all sectors now ground to a halt. The Paraguayans took the initiative, which they would hold for the rest of the war.

In August 1933, the Paraguayans overran Fortin Alihuata, capturing thousands of Bolivian soldiers and large supplies of weapons. The remaining Bolivian units in the area withdrew to new defensive lines at Muñoz and Ballivian. In December 1933, a ceasefire came into effect, scheduled to last for twenty days. Fighting ceased, allowing the two sides to meet and try to work out a peaceful solution. Paraguay hoped to negotiate favorably because of its victories in the battlefield. However, in early January 1934, the ceasefire lapsed with no settlement reached.

The Paraguayan forces launched new offensives against the Bolivians who had taken advantage of the lull in the fighting to send more troops and weapons to the front lines. By early April 1934, the Paraguayans had captured Muñoz and Cañada Tarija, thereby wresting control of much of central and all of southern Chaco.

By November 1934, El Carmen and Ballivian also had fallen to the Paraguayans; nearly the whole disputed territory was in Paraguay's possession. And with its capture of Ybobobo in December 1934, the Paraguayan Army was within striking distance of Villa Montes and the Bolivian oil fields at the Andes foothills.

The fighting shifted to the Andes foothills, where the results differed. In February 1935, the Paraguayans attacked Villa Montes but were repulsed with heavy losses. Another Paraguayan offensive in March on the Camiri oil fields was foiled, as was the attempt at

Charagua the following month. Thereafter, the Paraguayan Army realized that while it had achieved its military objectives in the North Chaco, it could not go any further into Bolivia without incurring heavy losses.

Map 28. Chaco War. Battle sites in the Chaco region and eastern Bolivia.

While some politicians on both sides demanded for the continuation of the war, the governments of Paraguay and Bolivia were alarmed that the huge human and economic tolls were bringing their countries to ruin. War casualties had reached 100,000 dead, with nearly 60% of that figure suffered by Bolivia. On June 12, 1935, in a truce mediated by the Argentinean government, Paraguay and Bolivia agreed to end the war.

The territorial issue of the North Chaco was brought before an arbitration panel consisting of members from South American countries. In its decision, the arbitration panel awarded 75% of the North Chaco to Paraguay, and the rest (25%) to Bolivia. The panel's decision also stipulated that Paraguay must grant Bolivia access to the Paraguay River, as well as to specified ports and rail facilities inside Paraguay.

No oil of commercial quantity was found in the region of the North Chaco awarded to Paraguay. In Bolivia, however, with its portion of the North Chaco situated adjacent to its existing oil fields, significant petroleum deposits were found and extracted. An outlet for Bolivia's oil was made by pipeline through Brazil, rendering the original plan of oil tanker transport through the Paraguay River undeveloped.

1932 SALVADORAN PEASANT UPRISING

During the 1930s, El Salvador suffered great social upheaval in its western departments (provinces). The peasant workers who lived there were members of the Pipil indigenous people and they resented their low pay and dire living conditions. These indigenous peasants worked in coffee plantations owned by European-descended landowners. During the 1880s, the Salvadoran government passed new laws that took away the ancestral lands of the country's indigenous peoples. The expropriated lands eventually came to be owned by a few wealthy landholders who developed the lands into plantations that produced highly valued, exported coffee beans. By the early 1900s, some thirty to forty landholding families owned vast tracts of the country's fertile lands. They had acquired these lands through government laws and the old Royal Spanish decrees, as well as through direct purchases.

El Salvador's wealth distribution was grossly disproportionate: 90% of the country's wealth was in the hands of only 1% of the population. The rich lived extravagantly while the poor practically had nothing; the middle class was non-existent. Politicians of European descent had a stranglehold on government power, and enacted laws favorable to the ruling and wealthy classes.

In 1927, a moderate government came to power and began to implement reforms. Then in 1931, Arturo Araujo succeeded as president and continued the reforms of the previous regime. President Araujo also enacted new social, economic, and labor laws favorable to the lower classes. More crucially, he legalized the Salvadoran

Communist Party and allowed elected communists to hold public office.

During the 1930s, El Salvador was affected severely by the Great Depression, as coffee beans, which contributed 90% of the country's export earnings, experienced drastic price reductions in the world market. Thousands of Salvadoran farm workers lost their jobs; those that remained employed were hit with big wage cuts and reduced food rations.

Meanwhile, the Salvadoran communists, led by Farabundo Marti, began to mobilize the peasants, promising them land reform and the return of indigenous lands. In May 1930, some 80,000 peasants demonstrated in the streets of San Salvador, the country's capital.

In December 1931, President Araujo was deposed in a military coup. General Maximiliano Martinez came to power and formed a military dictatorship. He banned the Salvadoran Communist Party and voided the reforms of the previous governments. He allowed the local elections scheduled for the following month, January 1932, to be held. The winning communist candidates, however, were prevented from taking office after the government nullified the elections' results.

In El Salvador's western provinces, regional communist leaders incited the peasants to carry out acts of defiance against landowners. Tensions between peasants and landowners led to sporadic violence, which were largely contained by local government forces. Despite their apparent affiliation to the communists, the peasants carried out militant actions to push for better working conditions and negotiate the return of their ancestral lands. However, the government believed that the peasants were communists.

In San Salvador, Marti and other communist leaders made preparations to overthrow the government. However, the plot was discovered by the authorities, who arrested Marti and his followers. Marti was executed on February 1.

Despite the loss of their leaders, the Salvadoran communists carried out the previously scheduled attack on the capital on January 20. Government forces repulsed the attack; with their defeat, the communist movement in El Salvador virtually collapsed.

In the western provinces, the peasants broke out in rebellion. In Sonsonate and Ahuachapan Provinces, thousands of peasants attacked many towns, including Colon, Izalco, Juayua, Nahuizalco, Salcotitan, and Tecuba (Map 29). Armed with machetes, clubs, spears, and a few firearms, they overcame the small local security forces by sheer numbers. The peasants then took control of the towns, where they destroyed government buildings, army barracks, and public works and utilities. They also executed about one hundred local officials, military personnel, and civilians.

In San Salvador, General Martinez declared martial law, first in the besieged western provinces and later throughout the country. He then sent the Salvadoran Army and the National Guard to the western provinces. Government forces were reinforced by private militias of wealthy landowners. Within a few days, the combined forces had quelled the uprising. General Martinez then ordered the destruction of all communist elements.

What followed was a campaign of annihilation historically called "La Matanza" (The Slaughter/Massacre), where government soldiers systematically executed as many as 30,000 indigenous peasants in the western provinces. Persons who looked, spoke, and clothed like Pipil natives were targeted; thus, thousands of other tribal people also were killed. In Izalco, the residents were gathered in the open, and after being brought forward in groups of sixty, were gunned down by machine guns. Their bodies were then thrown on the roadsides. Rebel leaders were hanged or shot. Perfunctory trials consisted of one question, "Are you a communist?", and the victims were handed down a guilty sentence, regardless of their answer. Whole villages were torched or demolished.

So destructive was La Matanza to the collective psyche of the Pipil people that they discarded (out of fear of more repression) their language and culture altogether, and adopted the Spanish language and clothing, and allowed their own integration into mainstream Salvadoran society. The massive loss of farm workers in the western provinces required the transferring there of many peasants from other parts of the country.

Map 29. 1932 Salvadoran Peasant Uprising. El Salvador's western region was the center of civilian unrest arising from the country's socio-economic inequalities.

For the next fifty years after the uprising, a succession of authoritarian, often military governments, ruled El Salvador. Then in 1980, Farabundo Marti, the slain communist leader of the 1930s, inspired the formation of the Farabundo Marti National Liberation Front, a Marxist guerilla organization that waged a rebellion against the Salvadoran military government.

BIBLIOGRAPHY

Maps

Collins World Atlas, 5th ed. London: Harper Collins, 1997.

Encyclopedia Britannica World Atlas. Chicago: Encyclopedia Britannica, 2005.

Hammond World Atlas Corporation. *Hammond World Atlas,* 3rd Ed. Maplewood, New Jersey: Hammond, 2000.

Cambodian Civil War

Aliprandini, Michael. "Pol Pot: Young Revolutionary." History Reference Center Database: World History – The Cold War & Societal Change (1946-1990).

Bergin, Sean. *The Khmer Rouge and the Cambodian Genocide.* 1st ed. New York: Rosen Publishing Group, 2009.

"Cambodia." *Encyclopedia Britannica.* Encyclopedia Britannica Online Library Edition. Encyclopedia Britannica, Inc., 2013.

Dunlop, Nic. Lost Executioner: A Story of the Khmer Rouge. London: Bloomsbury, 2005.

"Indochina Wars." Encyclopedia Britannica. Encyclopedia Britannica Online Library Edition. Encyclopedia Britannica, Inc., 2013.

"Khmer Rouge." *Columbia Electronic Encyclopedia* 6th ed. June 2013.

McCarthy, Terry. "The Butcher of Cambodia." *Time* 151.16 (April 27, 1998): p.40.

"Vietnam Conquers Cambodia." Great Events, 1977-1982, vol. 8, p. 1033. World History – The Cold War and Societal Change (1946-1990).

Vietnamese Invasion of Cambodia

Deac, Wilfred P. *Road to the Killing Fields: The Cambodian War of 1970-1975*. College Station, Texas: A & M University Press, 1997.

Hood, Steven J. *Dragons Entangled: Indochina and the China-Vietnam War*. Armonk, New York: M. E. Sharpe, 1992.

"Indochina Wars." *Encyclopedia Britannica*. Encyclopedia Britannica Online Library Edition. Encyclopedia Britannica, Inc., 2013.

"Pol Pot." Columbia Electronic Encyclopedia, 6th Edition. June 2013.

Vincent, Steven. "At the Killing Fields." *Midwest Quarterly*. 38.3 (Spring 1997): 247-256.

Widyono, Benny. *Dancing in Shadows: The Khmer Rouge and the United Nations in Cambodia*. Lanham, Maryland: Rowman & Littlefield Publishers, 2008.

Chinese Civil War

Crouch, Gregory. "The Shanghai Gambit." *World War II* 28.1 (May/June 2013): 52-59.

Cushing, Jeffrey. "Great Trails on the Long March. *Military History* 21.2 (June 2004): 58-64.

"International Relations, 20th Century." *Encyclopedia Britannica*. Encyclopedia Britannica Online Library Edition. Encyclopedia Britannica, Inc., 2013.

Kim, Donggil. "Stalin and the Chinese Civil War." *Cold War History* 10.2 (May 2010): 185-202.

Lin, Hsiao-Ting. "War, Leadership and Ethnopolitics: Chiang Kai-shek and China's Frontiers, 1941-1945." *Journal of Contemporary China*. 18.59 (March 2009): 201-217.

Lynch, Michael J. *The Chinese Civil War of 1945-49*. Oxford, Long Island City, New York: Osprey Publishers, 2010.

"Mao Zedong." *Columbia Electronic Encyclopedia*, 6th ed. June 2013.

Westad, Odd Arne. *Decisive Encounters: The Chinese Civil War, 1946-1950*. Stanford, California: Stanford University Press, 2003.

Yi-Huan Kan, Francis. "The Irreconcilable China Rival Regimes and the Weakening of the Policies of Neutrality of the Great Powers." *Civil Wars* 3.4 (Winter 2000): 85-104.

Landing Operation on Hainan Island

"Break Up Attempt to Invade Hainan: Chinese Nationalists Say Many Junks were Bombed." *Lawrence Journal – World*, January 7, 1950.

"Chinese Communists Land on Hainan Island." *Cairns Post*, January 13, 1950. Retrieved on August 24, 2013 from http://nla.gov.au/nla.news-article42653511.

"Hainan Island Invasion." *Cairns Post*, March 29, 1950. Retrieved August 24, 2013, from http://nla.gov.au/nla.news-article42662076

"Hainan Falls." *Time Magazine* 55.18 (May 1950): 30.

"Invasion Junks Sunk: Nationalist Planes Attack Fleet Massed for Hainan Assault." *Reading Eagle*, January 30, 1950.

Anglo-Afghan War of 1919

"Afghanistan's Fateful Border." *Wilson Quarterly* 35.4 (Autumn 2011): 69-70.

"Anglo-Afghan War." *Encyclopedia Britannica*. Encyclopedia Britannica Online Library Edition. Encyclopedia Britannica, Inc. 2013.

Baker, K. J. A. *A Short History of Eighty Wars and Conflicts in Afghanistan and the NorthWest Frontier, 1839-2011*. 1st ed. Kenthurst, N. S. W., Australia: Rosenberg Publishing, 2011.

Barfield, Thomas J. *Afghanistan: A Cultural and Political History*. Princeton: Princeton University Press, 2010.

"Country Report: Afghanistan." *Background Notes on Countries of the World*. April 2005: p.3.

Fromkin, David. "The Great Game in Asia." *Foreign Affairs* 58.4 (Spring 1980): p. 936.

Lloyd, David. "The Afghan Quagmire." *History Today* 59.12 (December 2009): p. 72.

Murphy, John F. "War on India's Northwest Frontier." *Military History* 14.4 (October 1997): 30-38.

Norris, J. A. and L. W. Adamec. "Third Anglo-Afghan Wars (1919)." *Encyclopedia Iranica.* 2(1): 37-41. Originally published: December 15, 1985. Last updated: August 3, 2011.

Qassem, Ahmad Shayeq. "Afghanistan-Pakistan Relations: Border Controversies as Counter-terrorist Impediments." *Australian Journal of International Affairs* 60.1 (March 2007): 65-80.

1947-1948 Civil War in Palestine

Dajani, Daoundi, Mohammed S. and Zeina M. Barakat. "Contested Narratives." *Israel Studies* 18.2 (Summer 2013): 53-69.

Falah, Ghazi-Walid. "War, Peace and Land Seizure in Palestine's Border Area." *Third World Quarterly* 25.5 (July 2004): 955-975.

Herzog, Chaim. *The Arab-Israeli Wars: War and Peace in the Middle East from the 1948 War of Independence to the Present.* New York: Vintage Books, 2005.

Morris, Benny. *1948: A History of the First Arab-Israeli War.* New Haven, Connecticut: Yale University Press, 2008.

"Palestine." *Encyclopedia Britannica.* Encyclopedia Britannica Online Library Edition. Encyclopedia Britannica, Inc., 2013.

The End of the Palestine Mandate. London: I. B. Tauris & Co., Ltd., 1986.

Vick, Karl, Aaron J. Klein, and Ashraf Khalil. "The Gaza Problem." *Time* 180.23 (December 3, 2012): 32-37.

Yusuf, Muhsin. "The Partition of Palestine (1947) – an Arab Perspective." *Palestine-Israel Journal of Politics, Economics & Culture* 9.4 (2002): 39-49.

1948 Arab-Israeli War

"Arab-Israeli Wars." *Encyclopedia Britannica.* Encyclopedia Britannica Online Library Edition. Encyclopedia Britannica, Inc., 2013.

Herzog, Chaim. *The Arab-Israeli Wars: War and Peace in the Middle East from the 1948 War of Independence to the Present.* New York: Vintage Books, 2005.

Morris, Benny. *1948: A History of the First Arab-Israeli War.* New Haven, Connecticut: Yale University Press, 2008.

The End of the Palestine Mandate. London: I. B. Tauris & Co., Ltd., 1986.

Bosnian War

Benson, Leslie. *Yugoslavia: A Concise History.* Houndsmills, Basingstoke, Hampshire, New York: Palgrave, 2001.

"Bosnian Conflict." *Encyclopedia Britannica.* Encyclopedia Britannica Online Library Edition. Encyclopedia Britannica, Inc., 2013.

Burg, Steven L. *The War in Bosnia-Herzegovina: Ethnic Conflict and International Intervention.* Armonk, New York: M. E. Sharpe, 1999.

Ching, Jacqueline. *Genocide and the Bosnian War.* New York: Rosen Publishing Group, 2009.

De Giovanni, Janine. "Possessed by War." *Newsweek.* 158.4 (December 12, 2011): 40-47.

"Ethnic Cleansing in Bosnia." *CQ Researcher.* 14.29 (August 27, 2004): p. 697.

Hendrickson, Ryan. "NATO's Secretary General and the Use of Force: Willy Claes and the Air Strikes in Bosnia." *Armed Forces & Society* 31.1 (Fall 2004): 95-117.

Kosovo War

Benson, Leslie. *Yugoslavia: A Concise History.* Houndsmills, Basingstoke, Hampshire, New York: Palgrave, 2001.

Ignatieff, Michael. *Virtual War: Kosovo and Beyond.* Toronto, Ontario: Viking, 2000.

Judah, Tim. *Kosovo: War and Revenge.* New Haven, Connecticut: Yale University Press, 2000.

"Serbia." *Encyclopedia Britannica.* Encyclopedia Britannica Online Library Edition. Encyclopedia Britannica, Inc., 2013.

Webber, Mark. "The Kosovo War: A Recapitulation." *International Affairs* 85.3 (May 2009): 447-459.

Younghoon, Moon. "The Future of NATO." *Harvard International Review.* 34.3 (Winter 2013): 19-21.

Nagorno-Karabakh War

De Waal, Thomas. *Black Garden: Armenia and Azerbaijan through Peace and War.* New York: New York University Press, 2003.

Gahramanova, Aytan. "Paradigms of Political Mythologies and Perspectives of Reconciliation in the Case of the Nagorno-Karabakh Conflict." *International Negotiation* 15.1 (2010): 133-152.

Gamaghelyan, Phil. "Rethinking the Nagorno-Karabakh Conflict: Identity, Politics, Scholarship." *International Negotiation* 15.1 (2010): 33-56.

Isgandarova, Nazila. "Rape as a Tool against Women in War: The Role of Spiritual Caregivers to Support the Survivors of Ethnic Violence." *Cross Currents* 63.2 (June 2013): 174-184.

"Nagorno-Karabakh." *Encyclopedia Britannica.* Encyclopedia Britannica Online Library Edition. Encyclopedia Britannica, Inc., 2013.

Panico, Christopher. *Azerbaijan: Seven Years of Conflict in Nagorno-Karabakh.* New York: Human Rights Watch/Helsinki, 1994.

Rasizade, Alec. "Nagorno-Karabakh: An Apple of Discord Between Armenia and Azerbaijan Part One." *Contemporary Review* 283.1701 (2011): 166-175.

Rasizade, Alec. "Nagorno-Karabakh: An Apple of Discord Between Armenia and Azerbaijan Part Two." *Contemporary Review* 293.1702 (Autumn 2011): 295-306.

First Congo War

"Belgian Congo." *Encyclopedia Britannica*. Encyclopedia Britannica Online Library Edition. Encyclopedia Britannica, Inc., 2013.

Feddarko, Devin and Peter Graff. "Waiting for Kabila." *Time* 149.12 (March 24, 1997): 56-58.

Laurent-Désiré Kabila." *Columbia Electronic Encyclopedia*, 6th ed. June 2013.

"Mobutu Sese Seko." *Columbia Electronic Encyclopedia*, 6th ed. June 2013.

Young, Crawford. *The Rise and Decline of the Zairian State*. Madison, Wisconsin. University of Wisconsin Press, 1985.

Nelan, Bruce W. "Zaire's New Order." *Time* 149.19 (June 12, 1997): 52-55.

Nzongola-Ntalaja, Georges. *The Congo from Leopold to Kabila: A People's History*. London: New York: Zed Books, 2002.

Serrill, Michael and Peter Graff. "Finally, the End." *Time* 149.21 (June 26, 1997): 44-46.

Weis, Herbert F. and Tatiana Carayannis. "Reconstructing the Congo." *Journal of International Affairs* 58.1 (Fall 2004): 115-141.

Weiss, Herbert. "Civil War in the Congo." *Society* 38.3 (March/April 2001): 67-71.

Second Congo War

Crawley, Mike. "Kabila and Africa's 'First World War.'" *Christian Science Monitor* 93.37 (January 18, 2001).

Nzongola-Ntalaja, Georges. The Congo from Leopold to Kabila: A People's History. London:, New York: Zed Books, 2002.

Prunier, Gerard. Africa's World War: Congo, the Rwandan Genocide, and the Making of a Continental Catastrophe. Oxford:, New York: Oxford University Press, 2009.

Santoro, Lara. "Carving up Congo as World stands by." *Christian Science Monitor* 90.178 (August 7, 1998): 1.

Santoro, Lara. "A War in Africa Recalls August 1914 in Europe." *Christian Science Monitor* 90.235 (October 29, 1998): 6.

Weinstein, Jeremy M. "Africa's 'Scramble for Africa': Lessons of a Continental War." *World Policy Journal* 17.2 (Summer 2000): 11-20.

Angolan War of Independence

Baines, Gary. "Replaying Cuito Cuanavale." *History Today* 62.9 (September 2012): 3-4.

Brittain, Victoria. "Savimbi, Bloody Savimbi." *Nation* 259.2 (July 11, 1994): 50-53.

Campbell, Horace. "The Military Defeat of the South Africans in Angola." *Monthly Review: An Independent Socialist Magazine* 64.11 (April 2013): 32-43.

Falola, Toyin. *Hot Spot: Sub-Saharan Africa.* Santa Barbara, California: Greenwood, 2010.

James, W. Martin. *A Political History of the Civil War in Angola, 1974-1990.* New Brunswick, New Jersey: Transaction Publishers, 1992.

"Jonas Savimbi." *Columbia Electronic Encyclopedia*, 6th ed. June 2013.

Kasrils, Ronnie. "Cuito Cuanavale, Angola: 25th Anniversary of a Historic African Battle." *Monthly Review: An Independent Socialist Magazine* 64.11 (April 2013): 44-51.

Leys, Colin and John S. Saul. "Liberation without Democracy? The SWAPO Crisis of 1976." *Journal of Southern African Studies* 20.1 (March 1994): 123-147.

"Popular Movement for the Liberation of Angola." *Encyclopedia Britannica.* Encyclopedia Britannica Online Library Edition. Encyclopedia Britannica, Inc., 2013.

"UNITA." *Encyclopedia Britannica*. Encyclopedia Britannica Online Library Edition. Encyclopedia Britannica, Inc., 2013.

Angolan Civil War

"Angola." *Encyclopedia Britannica*. Encyclopedia Britannica Online Library Edition. Encyclopedia Britannica, Inc., 2013.

Castro, Alfred E. "The Forgotten War of Angola." *America* 169.19 (December 11, 1993): 6-7.

Falk, Pamela S. "Cuba in Africa." *Foreign Affairs* 65.5 (Summer 1987): 1077-1096.

Foss, Clive. "Cuba's African Adventures." *History Today* 60.3 (March 2010): 10-16.

James, W. Martin. *A Political History of the Civil War in Angola, 1974-1990*. New Brunswick, New Jersey: Transaction Publishers, 1992.

"Jonas Savimbi." *Encyclopedia Britannica*. Encyclopedia Britannica Online Library Edition. Encyclopedia Britannica, Inc., 2013.

Sayagues, Mercedes. "The Siege of Cuito." *Africa Report* 39.1 (January/February 1994): 17-20.

United States Occupation of Nicaragua, 1912-1933

"Bluefields." *Encyclopedia Britannica*. Encyclopedia Britannica Online Library Edition. Encyclopedia Britannica, Inc., 2013.

"Bluefields." *Columbia Electronic Encyclopedia*, 6th ed. June 2013.

"Dollar Diplomacy." *Encyclopedia Britannica*. Encyclopedia Britannica Online Library Edition. Encyclopedia Britannica, Inc., 2013.

Musicant, Ivan. "Intervention." *American History* 29.6 (February/March 1995): 28-40.

Football War

Booth, John A. *Understanding Central America: Global Forces, Rebellion, and Change*. Boulder, Colorado: Westview Press, 2010.

Cooper, Tom and Coelich March. "El Salvador vs. Honduras, 1969: The 100-Hour War." *Air Combat Information Group* (acig.org). Taken from http://www.acig.org/artman/publish/article_156.shtml

"El Salvador." *Encyclopedia Britannica.* Encyclopedia Britannica Online Library Edition. Encyclopedia Britannica, Inc., 2013.

"Honduras." *Encyclopedia Britannica.* Encyclopedia Britannica Online Library Edition. Encyclopedia Britannica, Inc., 2013.

Dirty War

"Dirty War." *Encyclopedia Britannica.* Encyclopedia Britannica Online Library Edition. Encyclopedia Britannica, Inc., 2013.

Foster, Kevin. "Disappearing Acts: Remembering the Victims of the Dirty War." *War, Literature & the Arts: An International Journal of the Humanities* 17.1/2 (2005): 252-264.

Ivanov, Georgi. "La Guerra Sucria – Argentina's Dirty War." *International Conflict Management* (March 16, 2010). Taken from http://www.academia.edu.

"Monroe Doctrine." *Encyclopedia Britannica.* Encyclopedia Britannica Online Library Edition. Encyclopedia Britannica, Inc., 2013.

Osiel, Mark. *Mass Atrocity, Ordinary Evil, and Hannah Arendt Criminal Consciousness in Argentina's Dirty War.* New Haven: Yale University Press, 2001.

Schmidli, William Michael. "Human Rights and the Cold War: The Campaign to halt the Argentine 'Dirty War'." *New Yorker* 88.5 (March 19, 2012): 54-65.

Chaco War

"Chaco War." *Encyclopedia Britannica.* Encyclopedia Britannica Online Library Edition. Encyclopedia Britannica, Inc., 2013.

Estigarribia, Jose Felix. *The Epic of the Chaco: Marshall Estigarribia's Memoirs of the Chaco War, 1932-1935.* Austin, Texas: University of Texas Press, 1950.

"Gran Chaco." *Columbia Electronic Encyclopedia,* 6th ed. June 2013.

Hughes, Matthew. "Logistics and Chaco War: Bolivia versus Paraguay, 1932-35." *The Journal of Military History* 69.2 (April 2005): 411-437. From

muse.jhu.edu/journals/journal_of_military_history/v069/69.2hughes.html

Lindsay, Ryan. "The Chaco War." ICE Case Studies. From http://www.american.edu/TED/ice/ice.htm

"Monroe Doctrine." *Encyclopedia Britannica.* Encyclopedia Britannica Online Library Edition. Encyclopedia Britannica, Inc., 2013.

Morales, Waltraud Q. "A Brief History of Bolivia." *Facts on File,* New York, 2010.

1932 Salvadoran Peasant Uprising

Booth, John A. *Understanding Central America: Global Forces, Rebellion, and Change.* Boulder, Colorado: Westview Press, 2010.

Brett, Edward T. "La Matanza 1932 Peasant Revolt." Immanuel Ness (ed). *The International Encyclopedia of Revolution and Protest.* Blackwell Publishing, 2009. Blackwell Reference Online (http://www.blackwellreference.com/public/)

"El Salvador." *Encyclopedia Britannica.* Encyclopedia Britannica Online Library Edition. Encyclopedia Britannica, Inc., 2013.

Keogh, Dermot. "El Salvador 1932, Peasant Revolt and Massacre." *The Crane Bag* 6.2 (1982): 7-14. Taken from http://www.jstor.org/stable/30023895.

Lindo-Fuentes, Hector, Erik Ching, and Rafael A. Lara-Martinez. *Remembering a Massacre in El Salvador: The Insurrection of 1932, Roque Dalton, and the Politics of Historical Memory.* University of New Mexico Press, 2007.

White, Christopher M. *The History of El Salvador.* Westport, Connecticut: Greenwood Press, 2009.

Nicaraguan Revolution (1961-1979) and Counter-revolution (1981-1990)

Brown, Timothy C. *The Real Contra War: Highlander Peasant Resistance in Nicaragua.* Norman: University of Oklahoma Press, 2001.

"Sandinista." *Encyclopedia Britannica.* Encyclopedia Britannica Online Library Edition. Encyclopedia Britannica, Inc., 2013.

Miranda, Roger. *The Civil War in Nicaragua: Inside the Sandinistas.* New Brunswick, USA: Transaction Publishers, 1993.

"Monroe Doctrine." *Encyclopedia Britannica.* Encyclopedia Britannica Online Library Edition. Encyclopedia Britannica, Inc., 2013.

Staten, Clifford L. *The History of Nicaragua.* Santa Barbara, California: Greenword, 2010.

INDEX

A

Africa's World War · 82
Agostinho Neto · 94, 103
Albanianization · 60
Alvor Agreement · 96
Amanullah · 31
Anastacio Somoza · 122, 123
Andes Mountains · 146
Angolan Civil War
    casualties · 114
Annihilation Decrees · 142
Anti-Communist Alliance · 142
Antonio Rosa Coutinho · 97
Armenia · 65
Armenians and Azerbaijanis
    purchase of weapons · 68
Arturo Araujo · 153
assimilados
    in Angola · 90
Augusto Sandino · 121, 123
Azerbaijan · 65

B

Baixa do Cassanje uprising · 92
Banyamulenge
    migration to the Congo · 73
Beijing · 23
    Chinese Civil War · 16
Bicesse Accords · 112
Bolivia · 145
Bosnia-Herzegovina
    main ethnic groups · 51
Bosnian Croat and Bosniak armies
    1995 summer offensive in the Bosnian
        War · 55
Bosnian Croats · 52
Bosnian Serbs · 52
British Empire in India · 31

C

Cabinda · 115
Cambodia · 1
Changsha · 20
Chiang Kai-shek · 15, 16, 21, 23, 29
China · 1, 13
China's Central Plains · 17
China's National Treasury
    transfer to Taiwan by Chiang Kai-shek
        · 24
Chinese Civil War · 13
Chinese Nationalists · 13
Chinese Soviet Republic · 16, 18
CIA
    involvement in Contra War · 128
    involvement in the Angolan War of
        Independence · 102
Communist Party of China · 14, 16
Conference of Independent States · 69
Contras · 129
Cuba
    involvement in the Angolan War of
        Independence · 100
Cuban-Angolan forces
    1988 offensive operations in southern
        Angola · 110
Cuito Cuanavale
    battle of · 108, 109
Cunene River Hydroelectric Dam
    complex · 99

D

death flight · 142
Deir Yassin Massacre · 38
Democratic Republic of the Congo · 73,
    79
Durand Line · 33

E

Eduardo dos Santos · 112
El Salvador · 133, 153
Emirate of Afghanistan · 31

F

Falkland Islands
    Argentina's invasion of · 143
Fidel Castro · 139
fortin · 147
France
    Involvement in Indo-China · 7
Front for the National Liberation of the
    Congo · 104

G

General Maximiliano Martinez · 154
Geneva Peace Accords · 7
Government of Unity and National
    Reconciliation
    in Angola · 113

H

Habibullah · 31
Hainan · 27
Han people · 13
Holden Roberto · 91
Honduras · 133
Hundred Hours War · 138

I

Indo-China · 1, 7
International Criminal Tribunal for the
    Former Yugoslavia · 55
Iraqis
    involvement in the 1948 Palestinian
    War · 43
Isabel Peron · 140

Ituri region · 87

J

Japanese forces
    occupation of China · 20
Jewish Army
    in Palestine · 37
Jimmy Carter · 125
Jonas Savimbi · 91, 112
    death · 114
Josip Broz · 59
Juan Peron · 139

K

Kalbajar
    fall of · 70
Kampuchea's Eastern Military Zone · 9
Katangese Gendarmes · 77
Khmer Rouge · 1, 3, 4, 7, 8
Kinshasa · 77, 82
Kisangani
    Congolese Army mutiny in · 80
Kivu Provinces · 73
Kosovo · 59
    recognition as an independent country
    · 63
Kosovo Albanians · 59
Kosovo Liberation Army · 60
Kosovo Serbs · 59
Kratie · 10
Kuomintang · 13, 25

L

La Matanza · 156
Lasva Valley Massacre · 56
Latrun
    occupation by Jordanian forces · 43
Laurent- Désiré Kabila · 74, 79
Leizhou Peninsula · 28
Lon Nol · 3
Long March · 18

Luanda · 89
Lusaka Ceasefire Agreement · 84

M

Managua · 124
Manchuria · 22
    Japanese invasion of · 18
Mao Zedong · 16, 18
Marcelo Caetano · 95
Markale Massacres · 56
Mikhail Gorbachev · 67, 111
MK · 104
Mobutu Sese Seko · 74, 79
Monroe Doctrine · 118
Mostar
    battle of · 53
Mozambique · 95

N

Nagorno-Karabakh · 65
Nagorno-Karabakh Armenians
    offensive operations · 68
Nanjing · 15
    battle of · 20
    dams destroyed · 20
    Nationalists' capital of China · 17
National Front for the Liberation of
    Angola (FNLA) · 91
National Union for the Total
    Independence of Angola (UNITA) ·
    91
Nationalist Army · 23, 25
NATO air strikes
    in the Bosnian War · 54
NATO air strikes in Kosovo · 62
Nicaragua · 117
Nicaragua Canal · 118
North Atlantic Treaty Organization
    involvement in the Kosovo War · 61
North Chaco · 145
North Korea · 30
North Vietnam · 1

O

Organization of African Unity · 84
    involvement in the Angolan War of
        Independence · 94
Organization of American States
    ceasefire in the Football War · 137

P

Palestine · 35
Palestinian Arabs
    refugees after the 1948 War · 49
Paraguay · 145
People's Movement for the Liberation of
    Angola (MPLA) · 90, 103
People's Republic of China
    establishment of the · 25
Phnom Penh · 2, 3, 10
Pipil indigenous people · 153
Pol Pot · 1, 5
Portuguese Guinea · 95
Prince Norodom Sihanouk · 1
Prince Sihanouk · 4

Q

Qing monarchy · 14
Quifangondo
    battle of · 100

R

Rally for Congolese Democracy · 80
Red Army · 16, 19, 21, 22, 23, 25
Ronald Reagan · 128
Russian Civil War · 65
Rwanda and Uganda
    involvement in the First Congo War ·
        75
    involvement in the Second Congo
        War · 81
Rwandan and Ugandan Armies
    clashes in the Second Congo War · 85

Rwandan Civil War
    refugees · 73

S

Scramble for Africa · 89
Shanghai · 20
South Africa
    invasion of Angola · 99
    involvement in the Angolan War of
        Independence · 98, 103
    offensive operations against SWAPO ·
        105
South African Development Community
    involvement in the Second Congo
        War · 81
South Korea · 30
South West African People's
    Organization · 104
South-West Africa · 98, 111
Soviet invasion of the Caucasus · 66
Soviet Union
    involvement in Angola · 107
    reforms in the · 66
    Support for Kuomintang · 15
Soviet-Chinese relations
    deterioration of · 10
State of Israel
    independence of the · 43
Sun Yat-sen · 14

T

Taiwan · 25, 27
Tegucigalpa · 135
Treaty of Gandamak · 31

U

UN Partition Plan for Palestine · 35
United Nations
    involvement in the Bosnian War · 54
    mediation in the Second Congo War ·
        84
United States

involvement in Indo-China · 1
involvement in Nicaragua · 117
involvement in the Angolan War of
    Independence · 103
involvement in the Chinese Civil War
    · 21

V

Vietnam
    invasion of Cambodia · 7, 10
Vietnam War · 1
Vietnamese Armed Forces
    strength · 11
Vietnamese-Soviet Treaty of Friendship
    and Cooperation · 10

W

Wang Jingwei · 15, 16
warlord · 14
warlords
    during the Chinese Civil War · 13
World War II
    in relation to the Chinese Civil War ·
        20
    Portuguese migration to Angola after ·
        90
    rise of nationalism in Palestine after ·
        35

X

Xuzhou · 23

Y

Yan'an · 18, 22
Yangtze River · 17, 23, 25
Yellow River · 17
Yuan Shikai · 14
Yugoslav Army
    involvement in the Kosovo War · 61

Yugoslavia · 59

Z

Zaire · 73

53376270R00104

5771 INDUSTRIAL AVE